Understanding Youth Crime

Humayrah Shazad

Editing, Design, Typesetting and Publishing by UK Book Publishing

www.ukbookpublishing.com

ISBN: 978-1-915338-59-4

Contents

CONTENTS

Outline and critically discuss the ways in which your studies have developed your understanding of the inter-relationship between 'deviance' and 'social control'.

This chapter sets out to explain my studies' evolving interpretations of the terms 'deviance' and 'social control', whether or not they work together or separately, and if they have, how and why. Prior to my studies as a student, I had little knowledge of the terms and what they meant.

However, I recognised they had lawful meanings to them. Thus, whilst learning academically as a student my mind was set on deterrence being an act of social control, an attempt for higher power to ensure society stays harmoniously together as it should. Without any infatuations towards violence or irreversible outbreaks of horrendous changes. On the other hand my mind was set on deviance acting as a technical term for a controlling environment that soon changed as I read further into academic studies. Both of my previous definitions have been ousted by the legitimate terms I have found after reading from criminological referrals. I now acknowledge social control as a logical term for wrongdoers, it is an act which goes against standard societal morals and norms as well as national laws, for example, criminals and anti-socialists (Innes, M 2003). My understanding of social control seemed intact, it just needed to be enhanced. Social control is acts such as formal (a formal act would be an act pursued through laws and religion) and informal (an informal act would be an act presented within education, families and local communities) laws, morals and norms, which are put in place to pursue maintenance in societies to produce reduced or crime free environments (Innes, M 2003).

My reading also brought to light that these theories are not natural, they are constructed; criminologists have labelled this as the social construction theory, this theorizes that forms such as social control and deviance are scientifically manufactured through a looping circle which combines truth, knowledge and belief. As a theory-based ideology, social construction theory contradicts positivism, which theorizes the belief of reality over manufactured, it believes certain objects hold certain characteristics which enable humans to define them (Innes, M 2003) – for example: a chair is a chair (positivists would argue we can call it a chair because of certain characteristics i.e. seat, four legs etc). However, social constructivists argue a chair is a chair because mankind said so. The circle evolved around social construction theory is said to be a maze in which politicians and lawmakers consider when putting forward ideologies towards the different classes, and environmental areas. For example, when politicians provide new laws and orders such as ASBOs, they are critically regarded by the opposing party as a means of destruction for certain groups, genders, ages. This enables opposition parties to gain trust and respect within masses. Taking the ASBOs into consideration, there were many issues outlined by the opposition party (Conservatives) of Labour (who introduced ASBOs) – Teresa May (July 2011) suggested: ASBOs were getting out of hand, there were too many, and many were uncalled for; she also claimed it would criminalize youths unnecessarily, it would reduce their motivation rather than promote their capabilities (Ireland, S 2011).

An addition to the ASBO's deviant label, is the formation of views which have been constructed around suicide, which during my studies, I have found it is somewhat classified as deviant – prior to my studies I did not consider suicide having been such an effective act, in which people would form deviant views attached to it; for me suicidal tendencies are something only the individual should be worried about, any consideration of help should be from family and friends, not the public. Suicide is something which occurs when the person believes they have seen, done and been through everything, it is a silent cry for help, the last cry which they are attempting to take. I also believed suicide was seen as a very remorseful thing for the public, as the movie THE BRIDGE (2005) has portrayed. However, it also portrays some of the negative feedback people give, which I find promotes the suicides' untold stories. They rather label them as misfortunate people, people who are attention-seeking, rather than people who are grieving with no ounce of help in sight. The movie THE

BRIDGE (2005) by Eric Steel, is a documentary movie about people who have committed suicide on a certain bridge in the previous year. They interviewed loved ones of the deceased, and also people who witnessed the suicide. During the movie, the loved ones portray the deceased as people who had no insight into the future world, one woman whose friend JEAN had committed suicide was told of having qualities of someone who was not in this world at the same level as other humans were. This again is similar to the traveller's story: if you are not seen as normal, or if you are different to the extent that many members of the public can notice, you are considered an outcast. Furthermore, those interviewed are telling of the surroundings of the scenes in which the suicide had occurred, and one individual states that while someone attempted falling off the bridge, the onlookers laughed and said 'it happens all the time'. Scenes like this not only produce negative views about individuals, they also contaminate what the individual is thinking, having a different mind or having personal issues with appearance or one's inner-self is not seen by the public, rather the environment in which the act has occurred and the way the act has been conducted is taken into account – if you are committing suicide on a bridge, where 1000s of people visit, a bridge where thousands of vehicles containing children, parents, and sane people, is used to transport one from one side of the city to another, the act is seen as deviant! No matter what the crisis is, people are not fond of having to witness situations like this. The Golden Gate Bridge, which is the location for the movie THE BRIDGE (2005), is well known for many suicide cases. The article (produced by Friend, T. 2003) has taken into consideration, and produced some top stories on some of the individuals who have committed suicide. Friend has established the Golden Gate Bridge is a main point on which people attempt suicide, it is mythical, in which people believe it holds depressive qualities, as they suggest it signifies the technology of the beyond, but also the failure of society. To me this saying is signifying that the technological world may have evolved, but the society in which it inhabits has come to a standstill, it seems technology has taken over emotions and physical human interactions, which people consider important, therefore acting as a suppressive barrier, thus giving the bridge depressive qualities. The Golden Gate suicide stories, as monstrous as it sounds, have been producing poems, some famous people such as the founder of Victoria Secrets (committed suicide in 1993) have also been known to commit suicide on the bridge, adding to its famous qualities. After reading the article Jumpers – the fatal grandeur of the Golden Gate Bridge (Friend, T 2003) and watching the movie The Bridge (Steel, E 2005), my thoughts on suicide have not changed; however, I have nevertheless become more informed as to why individuals may form such negative views about people who have committed suicide, the state in which the act occurred, in addition with influential negative publication promotes the negative thoughts formed around suicide. This supports statements in which deviant acts are developed through influential people, who wish to keep societies socially controlled; this promptly eliminates outbreaks of wrong behaviour which is decided by them.

Another subject issue of perception, which I believe has close relations to the subject of suicide, is the social construction of rape and the views people hold as groups or as individuals on the culture of genders. Rape has always been a means of creating fear within females, this forces them to conform to the agendas in which they prevail, e.g. women belong in the kitchen, and women should be pursuing their behaviours around the marital status they wish to hold with men. This perception of women has been founded through many eras before us, women were seen as vulnerable and inferior to men, they were seen as possessions of a man, and if not that then nothing. In the 18th and 19th century, the rape of a woman or child was known to be a violation of the property of the husband or father, thus allowing women to live in solitude, condemning them of their feelings towards the behaviour they encountered and in turn receiving minimal opportunities for justice. The issues of rape, justice and views have been reformed in some parts; however, minds are still baffling about what to believe and what to not believe. Young states this more clearly, where he suggests: there is a constant problematic changing and contested nature of crime and social problems (Young 1999, p40 martial rape 1991). This to me enacts the situations around what people believe. Many things can influence what people believe and what they want to believe; some people think something is not a crime. However, if many people or if those working in the Justice system state something is wrong, one may feel it necessary to alter the mind to believe so, eliminating their personal beliefs. I believe similar things happen often in crises such as rape and suicide views. Rape can be used in many ways, as examples or as moral panics ultimately leading to constant fear. This controls the extent women can lead their lives too, it also may condemn many men to keeping closed emotions, due to their fear of what society may think. People may have experienced some crimes first hand. However people create perceptions based on what they see, hear and read, and this directly influences what they initially believe; they could believe something else but if they see something that seems legitimate, they will turn, and may question their own views, which creates such things as rape myths... Rape myths I believe are assumptions of appearance and nature, where the victim is considered to be blamed for being raped. Some examples of rape myths are: women are raped outside after dark; women who are drunk cannot accuse someone of rape as being drunk alters your brain's functionality; rape needs to be evident – having no scars means you were not raped and if you are a man and you are raped you are gay. Rape myths are created to help representatives to allocate fear within communities, thus producing social conformity. These conformities are usually something which no-one really questions, something I believe is not questioned enough and those who do question are simply then ignored, just because the majority believe otherwise. However, the function of the conformity they wish to issue between the community changes culturally. For example, the case of a young Indian college student, raped on her journey home, wearing westernized clothes, by multiple men, in broad daylight. The severity of the case touched the nation's hearts, they wished for change. However, the convicted claimed, I did this because the victim enticed me, she wore the clothes of a westernised women, I just fell in her trap, she called it on herself. Due to this one comment of the convicted, the nation changed; they forgot the pain she must have gone through, then started to conform girls: do not use public transport, do not wear such clothes, do not go to college, stay at home so we know you're safe. The girl was just a bad girl, she brought it on herself, and this is what happens when you wear such clothes, dress modestly. (*http://www.theguardian. com/film/india-s-daughter* Accessed: 19/03/16) Such rape myths create many impacts. They produce set views on how genders should behave, and what a criminal act should be. They refrain girls from being who they are and what they want to be. They also deny men of emotional behaviour from criminal encounters, they conform men and women to something socially constructed. I believe this only produces harmful distant behaviours within communities, especially of individuals seeking difference from what the norms are, thus deeming them deviant. It also suppresses questions from arising, such as why can't men be raped without being gay, why are men seen as monsters mainly in the media? Women could be called prostitutes and men could be seen as gay due to depressing behaviours, which the media has chosen to portray as deviant; characteristics are thus questioned, victims cannot attain closure. The media holds a very high influential podium for power to seep into people's everyday lives, this socially controls the communities to the power's pleasing levels; they aim for authority at the cost of the minority.

In conclusion, my interpretation of many terms and understandings have changed thoroughly from being taught in this module. I have found social control and deviance indefinitely marry together. The possession of skills to propose deviant acts in order to obtain social control, are found within the powerful, thus concluding the social construction theory of knowledge, truth and belief (Innes, M 2003) are true when providing power to the beneficiary. The powerful possess and produce knowledge, and contradicts the truth in order to create beliefs. This enable grounds for inflicting rules and regulations, and those who condone such behaviour are portrayed as insolent, and labelled accordingly as deviant actors. The power of the minority, infatuates the majority. The positions held by the minority i.e. politicians, is unquestionable according to the majority. Thus leaving the minority to choose what is to be controlled, to even choose whether things need to be controlled at all. Thus proving the manufacturing of social control. Which produces the existence of deviance. If social control, i.e. laws, norms, was not a thing, there would be no law breaking, no-one to be ousted and labelled as deviant. The providence and enforcement of law and orders, inflicted by power, create established and hard breaking societies. The infatuations imposed on society enables grounds for diffusion. Thus promoting stability for elite members to grow and the 'others' to remain at the bottom. This platforms, upholds the conflict of segregated communities/societies and concretes the social statuses. Prompting the usage and defiance of social control; allowing the powerful to stay at the top; securing their skills, and largely instigating the life of human nature they wish to oppose. Contamination of the skills causes loss therefore defying grounds of fear, and wrongdoing is a necessity to keeping their privileges and hypnotic strategies safe. On the same note, I feel that social control plays a stronger role in the inter-relationship of deviance and itself. As the importance of what is made means more when someone wants to break it. Overall I feel the inter-relationship of 'social control' and 'deviance' is significant. As I consider that one without the other will not affect society, as how the two together, do.

Bibliography

Friend, T (2003). Jumpers – The Fatal Grandeur of the Golden Gate Bridge (online) *http://www.newyorker.com/magazine/2003/10/13/jumpers* [accessed: 04/01/2015]

Innes, M (2003). *" the argument" in understanding social control: Deviance, Crime and Social Order.* Buckingham: Open University Press

Ireland, S (2011). ASBOs are dead, long live ASBOs. Criminal Justice Matters. 8(3), 26-27

The Bridge. (2005) [film] San-Francisco: Steel, E

Udwin, L (2015). Nalendra Modi must lift the ban on my film about rape in India (online) *http://www.theguardian.com/film/india-s-daughter* [date accessed: 20/03/2016]

(Young 1999, p.40)... Marital rape-1991

Youth Crime

This essay discusses the influences the media may have on youth crime. Furthermore, this essay sets out to inform how the media influences youth crimes, and impacts society using the theories of 'negative social labelling' and 'moral panic'. 'Negative social labelling' is the idea that people's words for one and other influences oneself immensely, immensely so that the individual may turn into the idea that the others have created *(Muncie, J. 1999)*. 'Moral panic' is the term used when a condition, episode, individual/group has been subjected as a threat to society/valued interest; this term is then further contracted with community out-casting and so on *(Young, J. 2009)*. Media representation on youth crime often results in negative outbursts during the aftermath; this can range from violent outburst to more subtle outbursts. This essay uses the case of 'Hassan Mahmood' in accordance with 'moral panic' and 'negative social labelling' to explore some of the negative results it may produce.

In the murder case of Hassan Mahmood (2014). A young boy aged 14 (Hassan Mahmood) was brutally murdered by 17-year-old Daniel Ekemba. The dispute occurred after a pre-aggravated confrontation between the two individuals. The pair exchanged aggravating insults over the social networking site 'Facebook', where they discussed the park meeting to 'settle scores'. The fight went from a boy 'fist' fight to an assault, with the victim (Hassan Mahmood) lying helplessly on the ground, with a single stab wound to the back. This then resulted in his death *(Mccarthy, R. 2014)*.

Whilst Daniel Ekemba was held on trial, police officials revealed his vile attitudes, pre-weaponry usage and pre-offences, one of which included the confrontation between Ekemba and an officer where Ekemba 'threatened the safety of the officer's children' *(Birmingham and Black country. 2014)*. As well as this, whilst held on trial, Ekemba showed no remorse and furthermore laughed when it became apparent that he had killed the victim. Ekemba was handed a sentence of a minimum 16 years. Whilst the case had already caused great divisions between the communities *(Greatrex, J. 2014)*, the 'Birmingham Mail' had battled with courts to order them to release the name of the individual who was covered by the rule of 'protection due to age'. The 'Birmingham Mail' had won the case, which released the individual's name (Daniel Ekemba), thus causing more pressure on youth groups to act out *(Lloyd, M. 2014)*. The release of Ekemba's name had stirred more tension between the black and Asian communities. Two communities where there is usually unity.

Criminology, the philosophy of crime and psychological behaviour, covers many areas and versions in the defining and forming of crime, social and psychological attributes to the human race. This language of academics is mainly described through theories (a system of ideas or beliefs which attempts to justify a situation or an action) (*Carrabine, E. et al 2004*).

In terms of the theories manifested through criminology, some offer better explanation to certain social ideologies than others. In the context of social theories, whether explaining the aftermath or the procedure of an incident, there is often more emphasis on some ideologies like moral panic, and labelling theories, than others and many co-exist with each other like the two mentioned in this essay (*Tierney, J. 2010*).

So, starting off with negative social labelling theory. This theory indicates that one's self-identity is immensely influenced by other individuals. Looking at the case of Hassan Mahmood, usage of negative wording for individuals such as 'violent' destroys the differences between the 'victim' and the 'perpetrator'. This not only gives acceptance to the incident being an accident, but it also gives individuals 'wounding' privileges to disturb the society's mental emotional responses, allowing it to turn into a blaming game which then may damage the individuals' identities (*Farmer, S. 2010*). The effects of this can reduce sympathy to both the families involved and it may aggravate the issue, causing distress in communities who are mainly looking for justice.

Negative social labelling theory also suggests social labelling gives room for negative terminology to be produced and used amongst individuals. In the case of Hassan Mahmood, inherently negative terms such as 'fatally', 'disgusted', and 'no remorse' qualifies readers of the news to believe it was a mad and sinister event. The news outlets adding on 'arguing beforehand' adds a normality of the violent criminality to the area the event occurred in. The addition of the perpetrator's past and pre-argument created the illusion of what people would class as 'normal fighting', which was not the case. This again devalues the scene and individuals lose sight of the real issues a case may hold, thus normalising actions and creating labels with it. This shows that the addition of words can change one's perception immensely. Something that can be seen as a 'tragic loss' could also be seen as 'normal thug fighting'. This also shows the heavy influence media may have on individuals. With just a few different words, media outlets can create a highly fictional negative story, far from the real deal (*Kaplan, B.H. et al. 1991*).

Another issue social labelling theory states is that social labelling acts as the excuse for deviant ideologies to be classified in the manner that they are. In the case of Hassan Mahmood, the perpetrator (Daniel Ekemba) was held for trial and whilst on trial a deluge of pre-offences were stated. One highlighted pre-offence where he threated 'an officer by the safety of the officers' children' was rehearsed over many news outlets (*Stanisalva, S. 2012*). The fact that the perpetrator could breach an officer's emotional barrier, indicated that this individual was very dangerous. When the perpetrator's identity came apparent the fact that he was 'black' added to the level of viciousness and dangerousness (*Richardson, A. 2014*). The knowledge of the perpetrator's previous convictions gives rise to more stigmatisation, as acting against an officer is not the norm even for minimally violent youths, but according to some it's normal for a 'black young male' to become extensively violent *(Farmer, S. 2010)*. This allows individuals' stigmas acceptance into society as the truth. Description and information like this gives in to the negative labelling effect that the theory discusses. It is a difficult process, but its effects are immensely hard to erase or change *(Farmer, S. 2010)*.

As well as this, negative social labelling is also said to attach itself more commonly with stereotyping. In the case of Hassan Mahmood, the victim, 'Asian male', and the perpetrator, 'black male' significantly adds to the stigma attached with these communities. Some of which suggest individuals of these communities are mainly violent and know nothing more than violent behaviour, indicating speculations of uneducated individuals. According to the theory of negative labelling, this case aids in further stereotyping of these communities with a moral acceptance from the wider majority *(Guéguen, N. 2001)*. This also gives way for 'normal statements' to be repeatedly used without a window of thought. Negative labelling theory also accepts that cases like Hassan Mahmood's with overly stigmatised opinions foreplay to a more isolated community. As seen with the Hassan Mahmood case, two communities usually unified, who are known to the world as vile individuals split with aggression and from that led the individuals on the outside to reproduce and voice opinions confirming the stereotypical chains attached to them *(Kaplan, B.H et al. 1991)*.

Finally, social labelling theory also indicates that media has an influence on stigmatisation. Looking at the case of Hassan Mahmood, the aftermath of this incident was that individuals stayed clear of the park as well as the individuals involved's respective families. The park is now a hotspot for gangs and crime, where before it received the bad publicity it was just a normal park; old, young, families, children and all would peacefully go there without a worry. Due to the media's portrayal of events, though it wasn't before, the park is now mainly a hotspot for drugs, gang violence and anti-social behaviours. This shows that media influences are so intent and influential that anything from an individual to an everyday object, item and/or area could be stigmatised (*Stanisalva, S. 2012*).

Moving on to the theory of moral panic. This theory is very similar to that of social labelling, in the sense that it creates a structured impact on society whether it be a bad or good impact. It is concise in the message it intends to send. That is a manipulated version of real events. The course of manipulation reveals a chain of moral disturbances, which media thrives on *(Farmer, S. 2010)*.

Cohen, a key thinker in moral panic, situates many types of moral panic. This essay will focus on the transmission of images and setting of the agenda. Moral panic theory states that the structure to cause panic starts off with a condition, episode, individual/group which is deemed as a threat to society or valued interest *(Farmer, S. 2010)*. Some examples of moral panics are chicken pox and swine flu. So, looking at the case of Hassan Mahmood with moral panic. In a youth against youth incident (Victim, 14, and perpetrator, 17) someone had been murdered. This is something which the community is not used to dealing with. The media rigorously lifted the story with new news almost every day, which resulted in the community where youth against youth was minimalised becoming very cautious of their surroundings and movements *(Muncie, J. 1999)*. There was an avoidance of parks and going out at night due to the fear of being targeted by 'thug youths', in particular, the 'Asian' and 'black' community youths.

Moral panic also suggests that in order to create moral panic, information portrayed via mass media is heavily perceived in a highly stereotypical manner. In the case of Hassan Mahmood the perpetrator's emotionlessness response deems the perpetrator as a dangerous 'thug' and a danger to society. The identity of the individual 'black male' adds to another level of dangerous *(Farmer, S. 2010)*. This then allows racist and stereotypical analysis of the black community to come to light. Views such as 'black people are violent, should not be approached and are born into violence' are echoed amongst the public. Thus, demonising the communities even more.

Adding on to this point. The fact that mass media, in this case BIRMINGHAM MAIL, MIRROR AND BBC, are manned, edited and delivered by far-right individuals shadows a professionalised viewpoint, therefore indicating that these far-right media outlets have leverage over individuals' thoughts. This also supports ideologies that far-rights have skills in which they can easily create an illusion from the reality it is *(Farmer, S. 2010)*. This is seen in this case, as 'BIRMINGHAM MAIL' takes the identity of the perpetrator to court. Once they had won the court ruling, they were given details of the perpetrator, which led to heavy news coverage. This was then followed on by more racist and stereotypical views; not only is this dangerous to societal structures but it also influences many social issues such as community out-casting and minorities drawing back from greater communities (*Stanisalva, S. 2012*).

Furthermore, moral panic theory indicates that as a structural movement of the display it creates, moral panics draw anxiety and/or alarming responses to the problem. The alarming response is often high peaked within a minimal time span; it is so high peaked that authorities must take swift action accordingly and quickly (*Farmer S. 2010*). Looking at Hassan Mahmood's case, the murder coverage added with the prosecution and identity process of the perpetrator, accelerated violent emotional but not physical responses throughout the communities. It came to points where individuals often classed these communities as violent/stupid without knowledge of any respective individuals (*Stanisalva, S. 2012*). The responses were further accelerated especially with youths who were 'street life' material, i.e. different clothing, ghetto language and a liking for destruction. Cases like Hassan Mahmood's just adds justification to individuals' racial/ discriminative views and actions. The effect of this was individuals would not speak of the case for fear of being taunted, and there was also a divide between two communities (Asian community and Black community) which usually co-exist well together.

Finally, moral panic states that the situation the structured movement may cause changes the ways in which individuals cope with and handle further situations. In this respective case, the victim's name resides with the park; as well as this no-one travels alone in the park, people who are unknown to the area or its surroundings are told of its anti-socialist attributes rather than it just being a normal park (*Farmer, S. 2010*). This shows that when the media portrays crime in such manners, the negativity level is raised; this not only shows the massive influential effect mass media can have on individuals' mindsets, but it also shows that mass media is so powerful that it can turn anything from an individual to a still object (like a building, tree etc.) into something it is not. It also shows they can do this just by making minor changes on platforms such as news outlets and these minor changes can be anything from different emotive language to style of writing.

To summarise, moral panic and negative social labelling theory carefully exemplifies how media represents youth crime. Moral panic and negative social labelling theory creates a sociological analysis on the powers and skills the media has developed over time. The skills the media have developed have a great abundance of ownership over an individual's thoughts on many aspects of life including youth culture and criminality (*Guéguen, N. 2001*). These possessive qualities the media holds against individuals is what the media thrives on. It is also what the media relies on whilst announcing news, this then further advocates them when manipulating mindsets to believe the story they are trying to sell. This suggests that the media's power and influence is unquestionable in sociological and physiological attainments. This therefore indicates that media is greatly influential in manifesting 'negative social labelling' and 'moral panic' theories in relation to youth crime. Its influence is so apparent that it opens platforms for more negative sociological issues like community withdrawal (small and large scales) and social dysfunction to manifest and escalate.

References

Birmingham and Black Country. (2014). Hassan Mahmood stabbing: Killer jailed for 16 years. Available: _http://www.bbc.co.uk/news/uk-england-birmingham-26837961. Last accessed 01/04/2017._

Carrabine, E. et al (2004). _Criminology a sociological introduction._ London: Routledge.

Famer, S. (2010). Criminality of black youths in inner-city schools: 'moral panic', moral imagination and moral formation. Race Ethnicity and Education. 13 (3), 367-381.

Greatrex, J. (2014). Live: Hassan Mahmood murder case sentencing – minute-by-minute updates from Birmingham Crown Court. Available: _http://www.birminghammail.co.uk/news/midlands-news/live-hassan-mahmood-murder-case-6901836_. Last accessed 01/04/2017.

Guéguen, N. (2001). SOCIAL LABELING AND COMPLIANCE: AN EVALUATION OF THE LINK BETWEEN THE LABEL AND THE REQUEST. Social Behaviour and Personality. 29 (8), 743-748.

Kaplan, B.H. et al. (1991). Negative Social Sanctions and Juvenile Delinquency: Effects of Labelling in a Model of Deviant Behaviour. Social Science Quarterly. 72 (1), 98.

Lloyd, M. (2014). Hassan Mahmood killer named for first time after Birmingham Mail overturns court ban. Available: _http://www. birminghammail.co.uk/news/midlands-news/hassan-mahmood-killer-daniel-ekemba-6976026_. Last accessed 02/04/2017.

Mccarthy, R. (2014). Hassan Mahmood murder: Seventeen-year-old found guilty of fatal stabbing. Available: _http://www. birminghammail.co.uk/news/midlands-news/hassan-mahmood-murder-seventeen-year-old-found-6648839_. Last accessed 01/04/2017.

Muncie, J (1999). Youth & Crime. 2nd ed. London: Sage Publications. 117-122.

Richardson, A. (2014). Family of murdered teen reveal killer's dad made emotional apology and was 'disgusted' by his son's cowardly act. Available: _http://www.mirror.co.uk/news/uk-news/ hassan-mahmood-family-murdered-teen-3100555_. Last accessed 02/04/2017.

Stanisalva, S. (2012). Media representation of youth violence in Bulgaria. Europe's Journal of psychology. 8 (1), 49.

Tierney, J (2010). Criminology theory and context. 3rd ed. London: Pearson education limited.

Young, J. (2009). Moral Panic. The British journal of Criminology. 49 (1), 4-16.

Working with Youths

Working in the criminal justice system

S15117315 | Social Studies

Abstract

This report offers an individual's personal account of experiencing a placement within an area of the criminal justice system. As well as this, the individual will draw upon relevant key theories surrounding the issues connected to youth and youth facilities, and produce critical discussions based on these theories in coherence with the personal accounts experienced. This report offers a realistic overview of a student's perspective on working in the youth facilities offered by the criminal justice system, as well as successfully identifying key contemporary issues within youth facilities, points of discussion such as: where these issues may have developed from and what category of social identification these issues may fit into, as well as possible solutions for these contemporary issues shall be discussed.

Introduction

This report shall describe and explain personal accounts faced during a work experience placement, which falls into the category of working within the criminal justice system. As well as this, critical discussions on the placement's lowest and highest attributes shall be examined against relevant theories. This will follow on to conclusions and possible solutions of any contemporary issues that may have been founded through this essay. The reflective report shall start off by giving a detailed overview of the placement and follow on to key issues or events faced during the placement which will help evaluate relevant theories into practice. This will all be tied together with an action plan and conclusion drawn out from what has been written in the report.

Before going into the main body of the essay, I feel it is important to include some information about the placement and how it fits into the criminal justice system, and some background information about why I chose this placement and how it may affect or contribute to my future career goals.

Background information about the placement:

The placement was at a centre which catered for students aged 11-15 years old who have been permanently excluded from public or mainstream schools. As well as this, they cater for primary school students and 16-year olds in a form known to children as college (where they do their GCSEs, referring to it as college allows for the children to believe they are heading towards a mature surrounding) (*Cobschool, 2018*). They also offer a wide range of disciplinary programmes for students who are on the brink of permanent exclusions (*Cobschool, 2018*). This centre, like many youth centre facilities, offers safe ways to re-connect 'damaged' and 'badly behaved' children back into mainstream society or a society where the children feel it is acceptable for them to live in. Centres like this not only offers guidance and safe areas of achievement for students, but to the judicial systems it is also deemed as an appropriate solution to troubled youths and their journey to social recovery. This method of somewhat rehabilitation is favoured more compared to other solutions like jail sentences, youth detention centres, foster care, social homes etc. They believe that centres like this better execute the needs the child may have as it puts the child in the middle of all aspects of what they offer and rarely allows for the children to fall through the cracks of the systems (*Cobschool, 2018*). This method also maintains better standards of what government programmes intended to do for youths. Although these sorts of clinical practices are hidden and not for every youth, they ensure that the facilities in place for these children are in check with government and the standards of the academical sector.

Background information about me:

As a student, many future career goals have always crossed my mind. However, one idea has always stayed in my head. The idea was to do something which could help a lot of people without being famously known for it (as I am a very shy individual, and I also do not like to take credit for anything). I was raised in an area with high unemployment, drug abuse, drug dealers, domestic violence, stranger dangers, illegal underage activity and negative stereotypical behaviourisms towards a lot of different types of individuals. So, the idea was to offer a haven that can be widely reached by many and used by many in a bid to help themselves or help others. I thought about the lowest of society; drug abusers, ex-offenders, youths, sex workers, women from stricter ethnicity groups etc. and thought what could be done to aid these individuals on a societal or psychological level. At first, I was concerned on how I'd fit the needs of all these individuals into one idea. However, I soon realized that it would lack in a lot of necessary things like the right emotive courses and the correct governmental protocols and guidance if it was to be done, so, I changed my thoughts towards youths and ex-offenders. I chose to focus on these two categories as these individuals suffer similar blacklashes from society (*Morenoff & Harding, 2014*). For example, youths (from underprivileged backgrounds) and ex-offenders both have difficulties in finding employment or getting into education, they often find themselves on the streets, getting into illegal activities or sleeping rough. In addition to this, sponsoring companies for society projects or charities would rather sponsor individuals from a category that society will have a warmer heart towards, rather than individuals many people would stay away from (*Morenoff & Harding, 2014*). As well as this, as I have closer connections to many ex-offenders from my local areas and youths of society through schools and voluntary projects, I also felt these were the categories I was most connected to. Therefore, I chose to offer a notion to help these individuals first. The idea I came up with was to have a centre which was funded like a charity. I am a strong believer in art therapy, so with that in mind I thought of other methods to help emotions flow, ex-offenders and youths are quite often on a rollercoaster of emotions, they sometimes need help to come back to contemporary society (*QuinnStreet, 2018*), so I thought emotive activities would help (so things like: boxing, music making, art, gym, pottery). Next, I thought of ways to help them find jobs, education or spread awareness of positive activities they could be doing. So, I thought of having the walls of this centre plastered in leaflets, colourful advertisements etc. and a help point of people to guide them on things in life or just for talking to so they could release that pressure of emotions. The idea was turning into a set vision the more I thought of it. However, I also knew that some parts of the ideas of the set visions were missing; this was because I was lacking knowledge of some important personality qualities of children of certain age groups. I find that with the different generations, even having a year's difference can have a great impact. I had already gotten experience from ex-offenders ranging from 18-50 years old and I also had gotten some experience working with primary school children, however I had little experience of some year groups between the ages of 11-17. Therefore, this work experience placement helped me in gaining surface level knowledge of the missing gaps I had. It also gave me knowledge on some of the more vulnerable individuals of these generations as the children I worked with had many issues ranging from family issues to educational issues, to economic issues.

The work experience

What the placement was:

The Link Centre belongs to a chain of centres known as the City of Birmingham Schools. The centres are located throughout Birmingham and are usually made up of students from and around the Birmingham areas (*Cobschool, 2018*). This schooling body is made up of several different organizations, such as: social services, police, the educational government sector, NHS and Ofsted (*Cobschool, 2018*). As mentioned previously, The Link Centre is a centre primarily for students who have been permanently excluded from mainstream schools (*Cobschool, 2018*). The school offers facilities for children of all ages including the infant 5-11 range and the teenage 16-year-old range (*Cobschool, 2018*). Their tutors are experienced in catering for difficult students and hold high mentoring abilities *(Cobschool, 2018)*. They also come from many different degree backgrounds, which allows for a smaller amount of staff members to work different studies at the school. This then allows students to familiarize themselves with a certain number of individuals, allowing them to create trusting bonds and defusing more confusion in their 'broken' lives (*see appendix 6*).

Their aim of moving forward together is portrayed throughout all academic and non-academic criteria and is also shown throughout their many projects. Some of these projects are intended to help students who are on the brink of exclusion, but have not yet been permanently excluded; examples of such projects are the IBC programme which is like a socialised version of the centre. It is a 3-6 week run course and offers students social and mental activities to help promote positive behaviour and attitudes during and outside of school (*Cobschool, 2018*). In addition to this, the centre's version of education is not like any other school. Seeing as its vision is moving forward together, they have adapted methods that work both mentally and socially, but these methods work outside the normal school boundaries. For example, ordinary schools have set timetables, they have few breaks and strict policies and rules which are not to be fiddled around with (*Cobschool, 2018*). They also do not allow for any wrong social, physical or mental contact to occur and if this occurs it is flagged up immediately, which is the main reason a lot of students get excluded in the first place (*see appendix 6*). In the centre it is totally the opposite: students can make mistakes, as long as they correct them or understand them as wrong. It is almost set out like a teenage pre-school nursery but with a structure of a prison-like building (*see appendix 6*). The students attending these centres have shorter lesson times, many breaks, and lessons are not influenced by exam board standards, they are influenced by mental and sociological impact. They do not have sets for different ages; rather they are taught together unless education is a reason for their behaviour issues.

Most of the students taught here often have some other issues besides schooling. For example, quite often students come from broken homes, poorer backgrounds, neglected surroundings, academic and non-academic disabilities etc. things that might be classed as deprived backgrounds. Therefore, this centre does not just act as a schooling method, but as a societal haven, a fill in the gap family and a place to re-create (*Cobschool, 2018*). A final point to add onto this, is the reason why the centre is the way it is in the first place. Their aim of moving forward together, is not just for the students, it signifies a tougher fight for deprived area children, broken societies and sometimes not all the times but for the tutors themselves. This school's biological-makeup reflects the deprivation in society and allows for the re-creation of the deprivation to be shown by allowing societies to come together to promote a better generation for the future (*Cobschool, 2018*).

My role:

My role during my time in this centre establishment was two things: one was an office or admin assistant where I would arrange student files, produce new files for newcomer students, ensure all files were kept in order and up to ethical and confidentiality standards (*see appendix 7-14*). I also ensured things were properly organized for staff and students (*see appendix 7-14*). In addition to this, another part of my routine for the office or admin role was to ensure all students had placed all phones, contraband items, jackets, and contraband food items in their lockers or behind the window with office responsibility (*see appendix 7-14*). This is also where I started to pick-up different children's personalities and began to question things such as why these children might be here in the first place. What did they do to get excluded?

The second part of my role within the school was a shadow assistant tutor; as the centre's academical part had changed since I was in school, I often just assisted tutors in lessons that I specialized in so as I did art and science during college and got top marks, I was mainly in the art and science lessons. I would also assist in lessons where there was an absent tutor or fewer staff members were available (*see appendix 7-14*). My time during lessons was made-up of getting students to do their work and for some of them walking through their work with them – this was mainly for the academically deprived students. The limited activities I had to do during lesson time, gave me time to do my own activities I wished to do, which was getting to know the students a bit better and getting to know each of their stories as to how they ended-up getting excluded, whether they like the centre and if so, why do they like it. I would also do some minor mentoring with the children during class times and during their break times. As well as these lessons, I would sit in with the centre's other programmes that were for students of different needs. For example, I would quite often sit in the programmes that were meant for children who were on the brink of exclusion; my role here was to again assist the tutor with their work. However, here I had more of a tutor role, as I had an advantage here as these lessons were more social and mental based. Therefore, what I had learnt in university had helped me the most here as I could relate theories and knowledge and put these learnt theories and gained knowledge into practice or execute it as an example of a scenario, rising issue, social issue that should or could be thought about before doing it (see appendix 7-14). As the centre catered for a small number of children and a lot of the time staff were short, so my overall role you could say was as a helping hand.

What it did for me:

Before my work experience took place, I was quite a withdrawn individual; this was due to various reasons. I was quite shy during lessons and with life in general. I never pushed myself to do more unless it was necessary. I was skilful in many things like art, science and mentoring. However, setbacks in life and a general distaste for socializing drew me into this shy world. With that in mind, academically, I knew quite a bit, but again this was not shown to the outside world as I would not showcase or reveal what I knew, my thoughts, ideas or anything. However, with some of this knowledge I had, I never understood how some of it worked in the real world. For example, during lectures and seminars of criminology modules often theories were explained in great depth, but I never understood how this would affect or in turn work for the real-life world. For example, Skinner's theory of behavioural traits (*McLeod, 2018*), how negative reinforcement and positive reinforcement works. The examples shown to us were from an animal's brain's dynamics, how animals would be if they went through negative and positive behavioural reinforcement. This theory of reinforcement was not shown through a real human version, so I didn't get how this would have worked until I had seen it for myself.

Over the course of my placement a lot had started to change for me. My confidence grew, and with this growth, things changed, I started to talk more, be more involved in the placement and outside in my own life too. This was seen most in university where I would start talking during my seminar lessons, answering questions I knew the answer to, starting off conversations with others first, and just being more socially active in general. I almost always tried to avoid conflictful situations but with this experience that changed too. Whilst at this placement I learnt that I had to do something for it to get done, and with this, I grew myself as an individual and this was through the given responsibility. Which in turn successfully worked out for me in the real working world. As well as this, with this growing skill of confidence, came the growth of the skills of independence, problem-solving, and the advancement of many other skills such as organization, time management and resourcefulness, skills I had but had not yet shown or had shown less. I was also able to handle setbacks better than before and was able to push myself to work to rectify or find other methods to fix those setbacks, or create something else from it. This working placement gave me a creative outlook space. The ability to really see theories put into practice. The opportunity to put my own thoughts, theories and ideas into practice, see the advantages and disadvantages of it, see how these ideas can be changed, or challenged or be presented differently to fit an array of personalities.

Throughout my journey of skilful growth in the placement on a personal level, I had also advanced my professional skills. This was due to the nature of my university course studies and the nature of the placement surrounding I was in. I had completed many modules during my time in university and some of these modules covered theories of personality traits, different disorders whether that be psychological, sociological or academical, youth culture/crime, youth in societies and economic theories that can be connected to the criminal realm. With this jointed knowledge learning curve, information learnt from the centre and the university had allowed me to become better at explaining things I knew. Therefore, through this experience the professional outlook was achieved. As well as this, as the students in the centre were made up of many different racial, ethnic and national backgrounds, I felt richer in knowledge of primary issues that could cause negative social behaviours of these backgrounds and potentially cause these children to be heavily negatively labelled, thus causing them to react differently, which in turn would lead to their exclusions (*see appendix 6*). This skill was mainly because I was in such proximity to the children. This first-hand learning allowed me to feel emotions and strains from a tutor perspective and a child perspective, which resulted in a more professional outlook as I could empathize with both the students and tutors and therefore give better precise answers to questions asked regarding children in societies of deprived areas. Also, the centre was quite involved with the children's outside of education lives, therefore, this allowed for better presumptions, reviews and solutions to be thought of or made for future centring methods (*see appendix 6*). In terms of how this placement produced a better professional version of myself, the key guidance was through the roles I had undertaken at this placement. I had the tutor and staff role from the beginning to the end, but by being one of the lowest tutors in the teaching staff's structure, the admin worker, I was able to feel how the tutoring staff felt regarding payments, handling work, handling 'difficult' students and handling the hierarchy of the tutors (*see appendix 1*). I was also able to feel the students' difficulties as for one I came from similar backgrounds to them; also, not long ago I was also a student of their ages and some of the situations that made them negative beings had occurred during my life too (*see appendix 2*). Therefore, I was able to connect with and learn their difficulties too, and this was better enhanced when I was performing the tutor role as although I was a tutor to them, I was also learning from them, which in turn made me a student tutor.

Critical discussion

Critical examinations of my work placement:

This placement, although very thorough in their commitments to allow the children to move positively forward in life, had some areas of ethical and educational work practices that may be questionable. Some of these are as follows: attitude towards newer staff members or trainee staff members. The staff members' habits in showing favouritism and normalizing behaviour. The centre's methods in teaching the effects of wrongdoings and if it really has any effect. The idea of IBC and its necessity. Their abilities in producing better working staff and the issue of having all children of different academic and social issues in one lesson, one teaching type and one method of education.

During this placement, some staff members had a broader approach to newer or trainee members of staff. This was found to be from the higher status staff members such as the head of centres and staff members who had been there longer. Taking an example I had endured during this placement, this point may be better explained: during my interviewing stage and the first week of being there the head of the centre was unaware I was starting my placement; this was because I had contacted an individual who was at a higher position than them and therefore, the admin officer had not told him beforehand that I would be doing a placement here (*see appendix 1*). As a result of this I was bombarded by a particularly broad individual who kept asking questions like 'what is it about you, that I should allow you to work in a centre like this' and 'I must think about the vulnerability of the children of the centre first, I must see if you can work here, I will let you know in a week' (*see appendix 1*). Not only this, but the work I was given in the first week or so was that of an admin assistant, not a tutor or a shadow mentor, which I had clearly asked for (*see appendix 1*). I was also told I was restricted to some of the work which I had wished to do as I was not an expert or a student of that course of study (*see appendix 1*). Even though I was able to do it anyway, at the start of the placement they suggested that as I was not a psychology or sociology student, I could not do direct mentoring or social services (*see appendix 1*). As well as this, this process of leaving the newbies to do all the jobs that they were too lazy to do sort of stayed with me until the end of the placement.

During this placement, staff members also showed immense qualities of favouritism towards certain students. This was evidenced by their punishment regimes for certain students. They often rewarded good behaviour with good treats and bad behaviour with good treats, so there was not a clearly defined line between what treat you would be given if you were good or bad. As well as this, some staff members who had taught at the centre for more than five years tended to normalize students' behaviour, which leads to tutors missing some important red alert situations and, in some cases, destroying the ability for justice to be served towards a victim. This was experienced during a time a student who had been there longer than the other student had threatened the other newer student with rape if she did not hand over her phone (*see appendix 2*). The student who this was said to be a grooming victim, she had stopped attending the centre after this occurred and the centre tried about three times to get her to come back, but after that, they just gave the student who committed the bullying a few words and that was it (*see appendix 2*). This student often told me and other new tutors of how he had raped students of the centre and non-students of the centre when he asked them for sex and they had said no (*see appendix 2*). When the behaviour of the student was told to members of staff for safeguarding measures, they replied with 'oh that's how he is, he is just trying to see how you react, so he knows if he can trust you or not' (*see appendix 2*). It was a situation where only the safeguarding tutors could sort out safeguarding measures if they themselves have spoken to the child in question and if any of what was said to another member of staff was said to them also, then this would be eligible to investigate; otherwise this behaviour was considered normal and not worrying to the safeguarding team members (*see appendix 2*).

In regard to treating the right and wrong behaviours, the centre was quite disproportionate in the way it treated badly behaved parents and students. In a centre that cares for the students' outside of academic surroundings lives and academic lives, the concern for their outside lives is seemingly low considering their aim of moving forward together is ensuring they have the correct welfare during their outside of schooling lives, which in turn would promote a better life in academic surroundings. This point could be evidenced by an aggravated argument I had witnessed; the argument was between a student and another student's mother (*see appendix 3*). It had started after the child supposedly verbally assaulted her other child whom she had left in the car (*see appendix 3*). After this, the mother started spewing hurtful comments towards the child like 'I'm going to punch your mom' and 'come and say that to my face' (*see appendix 3*). It was amazing to see how the children of the centre banded together and knew their lawful rights; however, the staff of the centre only defused the situation and never got around to talking sense or issuing punishments to those who were involved with the argument (*see appendix 3*). Rather they just excluded the child and said nothing to the mother (*see appendix 3*).

In terms of academical offerings, the centre offers a 3-6-week course for outside of the centre children who are on the brink of exclusion (*see appendix 4*). This allows for more children who need social, mental and academic support to be reached (*see appendix 4*). This course offers some of the children of these centres and others to really question their surroundings and tell of experiences they have had; this then allows for the tutors of the course to contribute sufficient information in the lessons that will then enhance better judgment, social, mental and academic qualities within the children (*see appendix 4*). The need for this course to continue and be allowed for all students is such a necessity that it would not only improve the abilities of those students but to the normal students also (*see appendix 4*). This would allow for a safe space for taboo subjects and non-tutor influenced discussions to take place, which in turn could allow for greater awareness of the world and contemporary issues around them. This would also reduce clouding judgment and create a different level of personal independence from children of these ages. However, as good as this course may be, both this centre and course do not cater for children who have other difficulties like anxiety, depression, low self-esteem and issues that would be classed as vulnerable disorders; rather they encourage the change of the negative or anti-social disorders, a part of society which is considered taboo in itself.

With this in mind, the centre's abilities to progress their staff members to become more effective members of staff for both the centre's reputation and the children's needs lack in self-motivation and mentoring from higher staff. The centre allows for staff members to experience different parts of the services they provide, one of which is having your own lesson, which you plan and can teach – they push you to do this in order for you to get a better feel of the students, how well they react with certain elements of education and how they do not interact with some (*see appendix 5*). They believe this would build more trusting bonds with the students, allow you to get more respect from them as they will see you from a different point of academical figures and it will also allow for the individual themselves to create future lessons or future conversations with different students with more ease (*see appendix 5*). However, with this in mind, often this journey of progression lacks in both suggestions from actual tutors and they do not provide you with any tips on how to relate the lessons to the children's likings (*see appendix 5*). This was evidenced by my own lesson I had where some of the students did not prefer my method of art therapy and thus disconnected from the lesson; in turn, I had no support from the tutors in what would work for them or what wouldn't, they just insisted that I try the experience out (*see appendix 5*).

A final point that can be presented as an issue for the centre is having all of the centre's children being taught in the same room, in the same style and with the same material. If the centre's aim is to move forward, the very idea of having all the children in one place to minimize differences may also be the reason the children worsen or show new difficulties over time (*see appendix 6*). This sharing of space may allow for the children to learn different behaviours from each other and may invite the learning of incriminating or anti-social behaviour (*see appendix 6*).

However, as this centre caters to students who are easily labelled as the unteachables, the matter of teaching standards is often ignored (*see appendix 6*). As well as this, the separation of more vulnerable students from 'normal' badly behaved students and then the reintegration of these vulnerable students may also invite the learning of poor behaviour from one another (*see appendix 6*). This may also lead to their non-schooling lives being affected also (*see appendix 6*). They may weaken in positive thoughts or the idea of moving forward if they are seeing students have more, less or having easier lives than them (*see appendix 6*). They may wish the same for themselves and thus act in accordance to the easier access method of getting to the desired place of life (*see appendix 6*).

Critical theories for discussion:

In consideration of the issues, I found during my time in the placement, some theories of criminology, psychology and tutoring can better explain these issues. The sense of broadness from the higher status staff members and their aim to produce better working staff may be explained through Earley and Bubb's (*2010*) idea of authority and professionalism. They suggest higher members of staff acting in such a way executes a line of structured staff members and when newer staff join, the broadness shown to them enables them to fall into their line of staff status quicker, producing fewer hierarchal clashes and a more professional outlook (*Earley & Bubb, 2010*). It is believed by Earley and Bubb (*2010*) once an individual has entered this line of the structured staff, their status is then buildable, and a warmer approach is given over time (*Earley & Bubb, 2010*). This idea suggests authority over emotions and can sometimes defuse the ability of the higher status staff members to enable their emotional awareness abilities to the lower grade staff members (*Earley & Bubb, 2010*), which then introduces different issues within the system, such as not being considerate of staff members' other priorities such as children, other work and socializing (*Earley & Bubb, 2010*). They also suggest that the broadness shown to new staff encourages the professional outlook most schools wish to achieve, therefore the act of broadness towards the individual may make them feel obliged to act in a manner fit for the school as it purveys seriousness and commitment (*Earley & Bubb, 2010*). It may also subdue one to feel the need to work harder; however, if the help is not given when a promoting offer strikes, then this could create ripples in the idea of authority, therefore allowing a hateful side of emotions to reside within the hierarchies, rather than a positive one.

Favouritism and normalization can be expressed through in-group favouritism and out-group prejudice, which will also show the encouragement and discouragement of right and wrongdoings and the appropriation of solutions from negative scenarios. The idea of the in-group and out-group is that the children of the in-group favouritism often have differed versions of punishments, if any, and this favouritism's reasonings can be connected to many reasons including racial, ethnical and social connection (*Aboud, 2003*). This can also lead to the social connectivity of the in-group and out-group being impaired due to an unshared space of educations (*Aboud, 2003*). This idea can be shared throughout the centres as often the students will contribute positive behaviourisms towards a certain tutor's lesson due to racial or ethnical connectivity, whereas in other lessons where there is less or no connectivity they may not work as well. This works for all ethnicities as the outcasted are fitted into an outcasted category and thus feel the emotional and physical wrath of this dysconnectivity (*see appendix 2*). This is further viewed as often tutors incite this favouritism and thus portray different educational collections for the different categories of the groups and therefore further this segregation (*Aboud, 2003*). As well as this, due to a social hierarchy of class, gender, race and ethnicity, often because of professionalism, tutors will look to purvey the causes of the issue that may have occurred and find a means to integrate any parents and carers to a designated in-group as this would defuse the need for a societal hierarchy discussion.

In addition to favouritism and normalization, another issue which could be presented as a risk for the centre is the idea of having all the centre's children taught in one study type, one room, one building. These children often come from low-class societal backgrounds and all have different issues – some have academic issues, others have family and social issues (*see appendix 6*). Looking at a prison theory of a toxic mix, this issue can be explained. The toxic mix theory suggests if all prisoners spend their time together, they may all counterpart in an idea known as social learning theory, which suggests that we learn from one another (*Ford, 2017*). This could be presented as an issue as it could worsen the likes of some prisoners as they may learn new skills and achieve different criminal acts

(*Ford, 2017*). Similarly, for the centre, if all the children who have different issues and come from different backgrounds share this space, they may worsen by learning from each other (*see appendix 6*). This can be mostly seen in the autistic children at the centre where they will learn how to behave from other students if they wish to achieve the same goal as that student (*see appendix 6*). This may encourage fake behaviour from students in a bid to get what they want and may act as a negative rather a positive (*see appendix 6*). Ideally, they have kept them together to have the children belong to an in-group and share the bond of being different. However, one could question if this is a solution if it may incite further negative behaviour.

In a final note for the critical discussion of theories, with regards to the theory of social learning alongside the idea of taboo subjects and outcasted students. What this centre offers to both students of the centre and students who are on the verge of exclusion is a safe space to be different. This allows for taboo individuals to come together and bond and learn from each other, not only negative behaviours but also coping strategies (*Bandura, 1977*). This learning space also teaches control of emotions, and the ability to rationally think in a positive manner (*see appendix 4*). This is done through the course of IBC, where they teach independence of thoughts, social awareness, social structures, how to be different and how to fit into society with these differences (*see appendix 4*). This is a positive for the centre and schools who encounter badly behaved children, as this method of schooling has the best results, it is mainly social-based and not educational-based. However, with that said, the system and centres have no regard for quiet, low self-esteemed, anxious and depressed children. There is clinical help for these children from psychologists and doctors, but these experiences are often daunting. Therefore, on a side note from this positive finding, there is no urgency of concern for the opposite of these negatively labelled children, which is the vulnerable children.

Conclusion

To conclude, my experience at the centre went quite well. I had advanced my key skills such as: confidence, speaking my feelings, speaking out loud, sticking to what I believe in and giving knowledgeable explanations of what I believe in. As well as this, the centre shone a lot of light on issues faced by these kind of institutions, in regard to schooling matters and social and psychological connections between youths, adults, the underprivileged and privileged, and societies in general. It also gave me insight into what could be done in connection to the advancements of societies that come from underprivileged backgrounds, for example: social activities that promote speaking the mind and creating social awareness on taboo subjects such as the IBC programme and methods that could enable an individual to produce a better version of themselves. However, with this being said, I also found flaws in the systems, and I found this is because of the government or bodies that these systems follow, these founding bodies are primarily the cause of how employees, for example tutors, see their students, whether they see it fit to care less or care more, it is due to what the higher powers believe. It also showed me the minimal efforts of 'help' the chosen government were giving and how far stretched resources were in these so-called methods of 'help' protocols.

Reference List

Aboud, F. (2003). The formation of in-group favouritism and out-group prejudice in young children. Are they distinct attitudes? *Developmental Psychology*, 39(1), pp.48-60.

Bandura, A (1977). *Social Learning Theory*. London: Prentice Hall: Englewood Cliffs.

Cobschool. (2018). *Our Aim*. Available: *http://cobschool-birmingham.frogos.net/app/os#!/outreach-2*. Last accessed 15th May 2018.

Earley, P. & Bubb, S (2010). *Helping staff develop in schools*. London: SAGE.

Ford, R. (2017). 'Toxic Mix' blamed for prison crisis. *The Times (London, England)*, 2(1), p.2.

Kelly, A. (2008). *Modern clubbing for the kids*. [image] Available at: *https://www.theguardian.com/society/2008/aug/20/youngpeople. youthjustice* [Accessed 15 May 2018].

McLeod, S. (2018). *Skinner Operant Conditioning*. Available: *https://www.simplypsychology.org/operant-conditioning.html*. Last accessed 15th May 2018.

Morenoff, J. and Harding, D. (2014). Incarceration, Prisoner Reentry and Communities. *Annu Rev Sociol*, 40(1), pp.411-492.

QuinnStreet. (2018). *Art therapy techniques*. Available: *http://www.allpsychologycareers.com/topics/art-therapy-techniques.html*. Last accessed 15th May 2018.

Bibliography

Anderson, M. (2011). Teacher and student perspectives on cultural proficiency. *Leadership (Burlingame, Calif)*, 40(5), p.32.

Keyser, J. (2016). Professionalism. *Researching in Accounting Regulation*, 28(2), pp.63-65.

Macken-Horarik, M. (2006). Hierarchies in diversities: What students' examined responses tell us about literacy practices in contemporary school English. *Australian Journal of Language and Literacy*, 21(9), p.52+.

Unknown (2017). Taboo subject. *Cape Times (South Africa)*, 1(1), p.1.

Appendix

Description;

- working with students of vulnerable backgrounds has allowed me to bridge a gap in personal experiences that I was missing. My future career goals in life is a career in criminal investigations as well as this, manifesting my own social enterprise for youth's in deprived areas and ex-offenders.
- Due to my area of residence and personal experiences. I felt I have enough emotive attachments with a range of individual types to pursue those goals respectively. However, I also felt I lacked in emotive and social connections to the younger age groups, commonly referred to as youths. This is a group which I would like to work closely with both of my career goals. I had little understanding of their social realities (my belief is that there is a big difference between youth generations with just one-year differences let alone generations with more than one-year differences). Therefore, I believe this experience has provided me with some memorable experiences, which I can cater to needs in varying circumstances.
- The Link's Centre (City of Birmingham Schools), is part of a governmental organisation primarily for students who are permanently excluded from school (primary and secondary), it is for residences of and around Birmingham. They offer basic education with major social and emotional aid. They also offer support called IBC for students who are on brink of getting permanently excluded, this is where an outreach tutor will go and watch how the student and school runs and offer programmes for the child to get back on track with their education. Students of the centres are noticeably different on a social and emotional basis's and at times may be difficult to understand comparing this to students of public schools, grammar schools, easier family lives, educationally accepted, etc.
- I believe the centre gave me the emotional bonding and insights I was looking to achieve from this type of work placement, I was able to overlook issues I had with some tutoring ways, and personnel, I was also able to put past my own thoughts and try to reckon, question and understand students thoughts even if I did not agree or understand it completely, I was also able to pick up some major schooling, social and economic issues and view their impacts first hand. However, I also believe I could have gotten more opportunities to produce more different areas of discussion and work such as providing a critical discussion based on a mentoring outlook if I was under a different course (i.e. social work student/psychologist) this is because as I was a criminology student I could not do what students of those courses could, for example; I could not mentor the children on my own, I could not give them mentoring sessions alone or shadowed, I could not do activities that I wanted to do with them because I was not a teacher, rather the role I was given was met half way with I wanted to do and half way with an assistant trainee tutor. I was working in an office and in lessons like a teaching assistant does, however, I did with this experience gain surface level experience of what I needed, therefore, I was satisfied with the role given as I was still allowed to bend some of my roles which merged me into a kind of mentor figure.
- The structuring of the centre was different to that of a normal school, regarding teacher qualifications, educational protocols, emotional/social barriers, teaching methods and prospectus's and so on. Some individuals would think of it as a fun method of teaching. However, you can see much more clearly once you're a part of the school and you're inside the building. This teaching method is designed to move forward together, the tutors here are more of mentors themselves rather strict teachers students often find themselves with

Appendix 1

Diary entry 2- [TWO OR THREE WEEKS INTO THE PLACEMENT]...

DESCRIPTION;

- Two or three weeks into the placement all is well. I have settled in with the children and staff quite well. Better than I expected. However, although quite settled I was concerned with one child's behaviour. The child was consistent in language that was displeasing and a flag up for stereotypical criminating behaviour. Some visiting staff members classed the child's behaviour as 'vile' and said there was a definite change from his previous behaviour, this could be because of his parental changes, going from his mom and sister who he loved the most to his father whom he feared and was a criminal himself, this method of behaviour was perhaps to retaliate but also shine a light that he has issues going on which he would want to talk about, it may have just needed the right person to talk to him.

- The child was very feisty physically, would throw excessive tantrums to get what he wanted. He would behave in a manner that some people would call 'extremely bratty'. My concern with the child was his use of language that seemed so natural for him to use. Remarks like 'oh miss, there's this girl (another child in the centre and another one not known to the school) I was getting on it with her and asked if she wanted sex, she said 'no' but I raped [this exact word] her anyway. There was also a case, where a rumour went around that he threatened a new centre child of rape if she did not hand over her phone. [the new child a grooming victim did not attend centre regularly after this and the centre knew about this] He would also only make the comment of doing things to girls too me which I found a bit unsettling as I a rape victim myself along with the characteristics of the child felt quite fearful of his presence near me. I believe the tutors knowing the girls past and how the child was, was a case of favouritism as they weren't too bothered with the child missing out on school and lacked in disciplinary action towards the offensive child to them it was just this is how he is, he is vulnerable and it is his learning curve, they hadn't had much to say about the girl beside she was difficult.

- I raised my worries with the centre. They just simply responded with 'oh he's doing that, so he can suss out how you are and see if your trusting or not' again this is to me favouritism and a lack of discipline which to me may be the reason why some of the children retaliated in such ways. Not much was done regarding the cases, he got a pep talk, and the new centre child was in a misleading way told to ignore it and just come to centre as normal, again diffusing from punishment for the child, and reluctance to help the new child as if she were so difficult.

- This child has a family background of a single parent. With the other parent sometimes in the picture. One parent persuades him to do things he does not wish to do (like keep robbed phones, claim the robbed phones are his and try to sell them on) and the other parent seems stern but also a lacking in the knowledge of nature in the son's personality. In his spare time, he is rioting in shops, robbing things, causing chaos [the centre is aware of this behaviour]. He also tries to give a vibe of fearfulness and power to the other centre children through physical stances and a tone of authority in his voice. This is worrying sometimes as he is placed in a nurturing group 'group for more vulnerable or academically less able student's' in lunch, break and class times, I believe his behaviour may come down to family dynamics and although one parent may be

Appendix 2

Diary entry 3 - [MY FIRST ENCOUNTER OF A FIGHT]...

Description;

- During this event, I was quite settled into the learning environment. I remembered the basic ins and outs of the day and had built a general schedule for myself of what I was going to do, or what I intended on learning for the day and from who. However, like any other day, it is always important to remember unexpected things can happen. A situation like that occurred which caught my attention.
- It is the argument between a child and another child of the centre's parent. This event includes an aggravated argument between a child's mother and a child of the centre. The mother had brought along her twin child of the child who was at the centre (her children have autism and ADHD).
- Whilst in a meeting with staff regarding the welfare of her child whilst at home and at school. The child she brought with her was left in the car and began making comments to the centre children (showing them a glass and imitating to throw it at them). The child of the centre had got fed up with the child's behaviour and spat back verbal comments (which is stereotypically expected for the child of the centre to do). Once the mother had come out, without questioning what happened she saw her child in the car was tearful. She began hurling verbal abuse at the centre child and became threatening with her postural stance.
- Arguments like ('I'm going to punch your mom' [from the mom]) and ('come and say that to my face [from the centre children]). Things escalated when the rest of the centre children began rallying up to defend the centre child. Whilst the mother under fury and the children ready to defend their ground it was chaotic scenes. Again, the staff did a great job of calming the situation down. However, no action was taken against the parent nor the child. There was no pep talk on social acceptances in mannerisms nor were there any set consequences for the child or mother's behaviour.
- However, I did notice how tight-knit the centre was after this event had occurred. The staff were generally on the child's side and were disgusted at the mother's behaviour however as professionals they had to suspend the child for two days and the mother had no cautions or meetings. I also had thoughts of how these children may be learning behavioural traits from their parents when it comes to mannerisms and social norms and rules.
- I did manage to get a few words to the child of the centre, and although realising his mistake he did not seem bothered to rectify it nor did the school encourage it. I also felt out of place when trying to talk to the student as I did not have much authority so I did not have much of a chance to get to talk to him properly (only like a five-minute talk).

Feelings;

- With this event, I did learn that although these children may be disadvantaged with behavioural issues, they are quite street and academically smart, they also have a great awareness of the judicial system's that favour their rights, this was shown when the children kept saying they know their rights to the mother and that she was not allowed to do this. This shows their versions of authority, they feel they are the children so they have an upper hand in things at the centre because if anything goes wrong the tutors and that mother break the lawful duty of care. Again this is showing how the teachers abide somewhat by the students as when this was brought up tutors became very friendly towards the children.

Appendix 3

Diary entry 4- [MY FIRST IBC LESSON]...

Description;

- The fourth major event I am going to describe. Is my first IBC lesson. One of the tutors who taught this course alongside another staff member was off on a school trip, so I filled in for her. I soon became a teacher[substitute] that would do the IBC regularly as a shadowing tutor as the other tutor could then attend to the centre's actual children as more staff were needed there.
- IBC is a programme organised by the centre for children from other schools who are on the brink of getting permanently excluded. The programme focuses on social and mental attributes of an individual and works to enhance the bettering of themselves. For example; the first lesson I sat in was based on reflectivity. The children had to make their own profiles in a PowerPoint format. The information they had to produce on their PowerPoints was based on a similar method to that of the Gibbs cycle of reflectivity.
- They also played games for 15 minutes as icebreakers before starting each lesson card games or games where you'd have to think for an outcome to be presented were the most popular types of games that were played.
- This course provided by the centre was one of the most dominant courses in providing key social and mental nurturing to children. It was not provided for students of the centre however the centre children had something similar for them, but it was only for children that were more sensitive than the other students i.e. learning difficulties, social problems, this method to the centre children was known as nurture.
- Adding to this, the centre children were presented to those children as something you wouldn't want to become. In a way using the centre children as a deterrence strategy to help persuade the IBC children that this schooling method is somewhere where they would not want to be, which would then hopefully minimalism their negative behaviour at schools.

Feelings;

- The IBC programme is the only programme in which I feel I saw the social, mental and psychological re-formation of a student that the centre was trying to achieve with their students. The most important thing about this programme is the questions and responses that were asked and given, life questions that were realistic to a child of that generation and age. For example; the tutor would ask, do you smoke? What would you do if your friends were smoking? Would you smoke? If not, why? The tutor would also share some professional but helpful advice/stories to the children, that would get them thinking, talking more. I believe this suggestive method is a type of therapy, particularly used for youth detention centre individuals. It is a psychological process where the mind has to work, think, solute to an answer, not just give it straight away.
- I feel this programme is most helpful for students of such backgrounds or difficulties and should be used throughout the centre, this is because this

Appendix 4

Diary entry 5- [MY OWN LESSON]...

Description;

- The last event I am going to talk about is my own lesson. I had wanted to try out some theories of art which I positively believed in, especially when it comes to personal development, social connecting and the building of the positive mental state. these theories of art are often used in art therapy procedures or even mind over matter procedures, it is more about the build-up to the outcome rather than the outcome itself, therefore, it focuses away from professionalism and more on mental currents relieving stress and easing the mind.
- I had two different lessons set up one was scraffito (scratching of the surface to reveal a pattern) and card art (creating blobs, dragging around a flat card and drying out the paper to find images and enhancing these images with your imagination and a pen) both of these art therapy methods is known as collage art. The children I worked with ranged from ages 11-15 (year 11's are sent to another centre which they refer to as college to create a sense of maturity), some of these students previously mentioned in my other diaries were of difficult family backgrounds, academic difficulties and general socialising difficulties.
- I found that the art methods oddly worked well with the students who have learning difficulties like autism and ADHD, this is due to the free-flowing mentality of the children with those difficulties and I also found they were more open-minded. Some of the other students found it boring or didn't like the fact that there was no end product (lacking in a final piece), which some individuals find frustrating as it mimics their own lives. This put me on edge, even more, when the tutor of the class started doubting my abilities. I felt more like a teacher figure which is not what I wanted to be, and I felt like a less like a mentor or an observer figure which is what I intended to be. However, I did learn the mannerisms some of the children had towards some tutors. A bit about their thought process in general.

Feelings;

- During my own art lesson. Students who I did not think would enjoy the project did and vice versa. I noticed a lot of the students adhered to their own thoughts, which left no room for thinking of anything else anyone else has to say. I honestly believe this is down to the centre's leniency with the students. They bribe the students to do well in forms of money/outings/presents. Which is all staff paid? I often get the vibe of spoilt children. They do not encourage to think about things in different lights and often have a rule of one way or no way, and if there is another way it is often portrayed to the children as difficult.
- Again, I believe this comes from the centre. On seeing how the children's parents behave towards their own children, other children and staff. The school acts as a sweet nanny figure rather a professional outlook where they should be getting real help from. Instead, it feels like their spoilt behaviour is enhanced and the centre's staff abides by their tantrums. This was definitely shown during my lessons, where the children got bored

Appendix 5

Diary entry 6- [MY FINAL DAYS]...

Description;

- This diary entry will be a round-up of the time in my centre placement. In other words, I am using this diary entry to generalise my time at the centre and speak of anything I found outstanding or anything that I wished I could have explored better.
- During some of my final days of centre, I was really getting to grips with working with the children. I was more confident, and I started to be more outspoken. I started to get stuck into aspects of the centre that I hadn't been really involved in, like the nurture group which is a group for the more vulnerable children to be in during lunch, break and teaching times and I wish I dabbed a little in the ethical sides of the schooling system such as the financial side, where their priorities lie when it comes to budgeting, spending etc. and also the schools methods of children confidentiality and social issues of the children.
- This is something I think should have done from the start as it showed a different side to the centre that I could have explored better and made more connections to form the modules I was studying, for example, these areas of the centre could have been explored through the use of theories such as the strain theory, criminological economic theories, social learning theory, toxic mix etc.
- As well as this, closer to the end of my placement I noticed a great deal of division between the people who run the school financially and ethically and the people who the run the centres such as heads of centres, school tutors, admin staff. There was no end of school/term meetings about tutor opinions about financial, ethical, social approvals of procedures or decisions put in place. There was a noticeable hierarchical structure, this which I find is difficult to see, as the way centre staff handle children is often the only thing the children know, tutors do not take time to the tell the students how the schooling system is worked and when the hierarchal structure makes differences in systems, often the staff are unable to explain the children correctly or explain it to them at all. This again leads to their way or no way. Which will in effect result in the one-mindedness and inabilities of the children to understand and accept change or differences in life, status, ethics etc.
- I also found a great difference between the teaching type and criteria for the different students, nurture students were more vulnerable therefore they were more lenient with them. The other students had a choice to behave how they wanted, thus the actions against them were different, this showed favouritism at its best, this is seen on all levels of education, however in centres like this, outsiders of the centre may be able to pick up on this more, due to the vulnerability aspect of the school.

Feelings;

- Even though the schooling system in this centre may have faults such as tutors show major acts of favouritism, different tutor teaching standards affect the children immensely and the different parts of the schooling

Appendix 6

▷ PHONE + "FACE TO FACE" INTERVIEW'S

LIMITED 'DAIRY' JOURNAL
(DAY 'TO' DAY)

START: 28/06/2017   END: 25/07/2017

HOUR'S: 140h. 25m

PLACEMENT: THE SCHOOL OF BIRMINGHAM   PLACEMENT CO-ORDINATOR:
(LINK'S CENTRE)   NOREEN RAMZAN

* 21ST JUNE 2017 [9:35 - 10:00]
GENERAL INDUCTION, STANDARD CHECKS (DBS, ETC), HOW
THE SCHOOL WORK'S. STAFF INTRODUCTION.

* 28TH JUNE 2017 [8:45 - 3:30]
CHILD SAFTEY TRAINING + END OF TRAINING QUIZZ
- HELPED OUT IN A WORKSHOP CALLED 'IPC'. IT IS FOR
CHILDREN ON THE OF EXCLUSION. PROGRAMME INCLUDES
SOCAIL / BEHAVIOURAL SKILLS LEARNING + EXECUTION OF
LEARNT. SENARIO'S + OPINION'S BASED WORKSHOP.

* 29TH JUNE 2017 [8:30-3:20]
CLASSROOM WORK SHADOWING THE TEACHER. ART
LESSON. YEAR 9 NOT STANDARD ART LESSON, MORE
MOTIVATIONAL. RELAXING ART. - 'IPC' LESSON, LEARNING
ABOUT OTHER INDIVIDUAL'S BEHAVIOURAL TRAIT'S, PEER PRESSUI
MEANING, EXAMPLE'S AND ONE SELF PRESENTATION.
- STUDENT PAPERWORK (SCHOOL PROCEEDURE, GOOD COMMUNITY,
SOCIALLY FOR EACH OTHER AND PUPIL'S, HAVE DE-BRIEFING
SO TEACHER'S CAN DE-FUME/RAISE CONCERN'S + MORE
EMOTIONALLY CONTROLLED WITH INDIVIDUALS)

Appendix 7

* 30th JUNE 2017 [8:20 - 3:20]

CLASSROOM WORK MATHS AND ART. GROUP WORK AND
INDIVIDUAL. NOT STANDARD AGE-LEVEL WORK. MORE EMOTIONAL
BASED WORK.
- I THINK PUPIL'S SHOULD DO MORE PSYCHOLOGICAL BASED WORK
I.E) ARTTHERAPY. MENTORING SESSIONS, SCENARIOS BASED THINGS.

* 03rd JULY 2017 [8:45 - 3:20]

CLASSROOM WORK AGAIN. LESSON'S MATH'S + ART.
GROUP. SIMPLE WORK. EXAMPLE OF EXPRESSIVE / EMOTIONAL WORK.
NOT NORMAL WORK. NOT STANDARD ACCEPTED WORK.

* 04th JULY 2017 [8:30 - 3:00]

ART GROUP WORK. YEAR 8, 9, + 10 AGAIN EMOTIONAL WORK
NOT PROPER ADJUSTED GRADED WORK.
- SWAT ROOM DUTIES. (CHILDREN RELAX, GET INTO LEARNING
            MOOD).

* 05th JULY 2017 [8:45 - 3:30]

ART + SCIENCE 4 8, 9 + 10. - 1BC ART PORTRAIT'S. EMOTIVE
WORK. PERSONAL + NORMAL WORK. - PSHE (SOCIAL LEARNING.
FOR CENTRE KID'S. DRUG'S / SEXUAL EDUCATION ETC.)

* 06th JULY 2017 [8:45 - 3:45]

CLASSROOM WORK + 1BC LESSONS. 4 10 + 8.
PLAYGROUND (KID'S NOT AS ACTIVE AS THE STANDARD
           KID SHOULD BE) KID'S HAVE ALOT OF ISSUE'S
             (FAMILY. SOCIAL, MENTAL, ACADEMIC)

Appendix 8

* 07ᵗʰ JULY 2017 [2.45 - 3.40]
CLASSROOM WORK, IBC YEAR 10 18
AGAIN EXPRESSIVE / PERSONAL WORK.
WORKING TOWARD'S SOCIALNESS

* 10ᵗʰ JULY 2017 [8.45 - 3.40]
CLASSROOM WORK. HAD OWN LESSON.
EXPRESSIVE PAINTING. WORK'S WELL WITH STUDENT'S
WERE'NT AS FIDGETY "FOUND IT FUN.".

* 11ᵗʰ JULY 2017 [8.50 - 3.30]
CLASSROOM WORK OWN LESSON. THIS TIME DID'NT WORK
AS WELL. FOUND IT BORING. UNRESPONSIVE.
- IBC SOCIAL SKILL'S
- NUMERACY

* 12ᵗʰ JULY 2017 [8.50 - 4.00]
ART ROOM. CHESS GAME (CALMING GAME WORKED FOR
SOME) ETHIC'S OFFICE JOB'S. FORM'S FILE'S, CONFIDENTIALTY.
ETC. SORTING, ARRANGING, QUESTIONING.

* 13ᵗʰ. JULY 2017 [9:00 - 3.45]
ETHIC'S (ABOUT KEEPING LEGALTY IN CHECK)
+ HELPING THE STUDENT'S EVERY DAY (WEEKLEY REPORT'S ARE
FILED)

* 14ᵗʰ JULY 2017 [8.45 - 3.45]
ETHIC'S + OFFICE WORK (CLASSROOM WORK STANDARD. SHADOWING)
- KEEPING PUPIL'S RECORD'S UP-TO-DATE ARRANGING FILES
+ FAXES FOR NEW SEPTEMBER PUPIL'S.

Appendix 9

✳✳✳ FINAL THOUGHTS ✳✳✳

▷ PERSONAL ADVANCEMENT'S + THOUGHT'S.
HAVING DEPRESSION + ANXIETY, I NEVER FULLY INVOLVE MYSELF
IN ANYTHING. I AM ALWAY'S WITHDRAWN. WORKING AT
THIS PLACE HAS HELPED ME CONQURE SITUATION'S I HAVE
BEEN TRYING TO FOR YEAR'S. THE ENVIRONMENT URGE'S
YOU TO GET STUCK IN AT TASK. YOU HAVE A SENSE OF
BELONGING AND RESPONSIBLTY. (LIKE YOU HAVE TO TAKE A
STANCE.) I CAN FREELY SPEAK MY MIND + WORDS
ACROSS SOMETHING I WOULD NEVER DO ESPECIALLY
IN SOME SITUATION'S THAT I WAS PUT IN. IT IS AMAZING
HOW A PLACE OF SUCH NATURE' CAN TURN OR PERSONALIZE
YOURE PERSONALITY INTO A MORE BRAVE + PROFOUND
INDIVIDUAL. MENTALLY AND PHYSICALLY.

▷ STAFF + STRUCTURE OF ENVIRONMENT. + CHILDREN
STAFF have TASK'S TO DISTRESS AND RAISE CONCERN'S.
EACH ONE'S CHARACTER'S SHOW THROUGH THE CHILDRE'NS
BEHAVIOUR AND WORK DURING THEIR CLASS. TIMING'S AND
STRUCTURE OF CLASS'S IS A GOOD PROMOTION TO GET KID'S
BACK INTO SCHOOL. MENTALLY THEY ARE A WELL ESTABLISHED
SOCIAL / ACADEMIC ENVIRONMENT FOR CHILDREN AND STAFF
A LIKE.. CHILDREN OF THE NATURE THEY ARE, FIND THE ENVIRONMENT
AS A SAFE ESCAPE, HELPFUL, STABLE ENVIRONMENT WHERE THEY
DON'T NEED TO FEEL EXCLUDED FROM ACTIVITIES OR ENVY "NORMAL"
CHILDREN. THEY DO NOT NEED TO FEEL OR GIVE LIBES OF VUNERABILITY.

▷ CONCERN'S
I FEEL GOVERNMENT COULD DO MORE FOR THE SOCIAL AND
MENTAL WELLBEING'S OF THE KID'S. IALSO FEEL MORE ACTIVITES
COULD BE DONE TOWARD'S EMOTNL CONTROL ON BEHAVIOUR TRAIT'S
(NEGATIVE ONE'S) I.E) ART THERAPY. GARDEN PROJECT'S, FARM'S ETC
SPIRITUALLY CONNECTING ACTIVITES. MENTAL /SOCIAL DEVELOPING ACTIVITIES.

Appendix 10

LOG BOOK (PLACEMENT EVIDENCE)

- STUDENT NAME: HUMAYRAH SHAZAD
- STUDENT ID: 15117315
- COURSE: CRIMINOLOGY & SECURITY STUDIES.
- MODULE: WORKING IN CRIMINAL JUSTICE (PLACEMENT)
- MODULE CODE: CRI6015.
- MODULE TUTOR:

- PLACEMENT OF CHOICE: City of Birmingham School.
  (Link centre) behaviour support service
- PLACEMENT ADDRESS: Jenkins STREET,
  BIRMINGHAM, small HEATH. B10 0QH.
- PLACEMENT CONTACT: 0121 464 3510.

- MEMBER OF STAFF WHO GAVE PLACMENT: NOREEN RAMZAN
  (Head of ADMIN, etc)

DATE PLACEMENT STARTED: 28/06/2017

DATE PLACEMENT ENDS: 25/07/2017

DATE/DAY/TIME	ACTIVITIES FOR THE DAY	HOURS	STUDENT SIGNATURE	PLACEMENT OFFICERS INITIALS	PLACEMENT OFFICERS SIGNATURE
28/06/17 WEDNESDAY. 9:35 - 10:00	- General re-run of how the place works (induction)	25mins	H.A.	N.R.	NRazen
28/06/2017 WEDNESDAY 8:45 - 3:30	- Child safety training/ quiz - Workshop both children on verge of exclusion social learning/skills	7hr		N.R	NRazen

Appendix 11

29/06/2017 8:30 - 3:20	- Classroom Artwork (colouring y9) - 1K class - paperwork.	7hr		NR	NRoja
30/06/2017 8:30 - 3:20	- Classroom 4 8/7/9/10 - 1PC class	7hr		NR	NRy
03/07/2017 8:45 - 3:20	- Class room work. maths, Art, Group work. Simple work	7hr		NR	NRajen
04/07/2017 8:30 - 3:00	- Art room group work - 4 8.9.10	7hr		NR	NRajen
05/07/2017 8:45 - 3:30	- Art & Science 4 8.9.10 - 1PC	7hr		NR	NRajen

Appendix 12

06/7/2017 8:45 3:40	- Classroom work - IBC Assignment 1hr - yew 8-10		H JP	NR	N Rayan
07/7/2017 8:45. 3:40	- Classroom work IBC - year 8:10	7h1	H JP	NR	N Rayan
10/7/2017 8:45. 3:40	- Classroom work - had own lesson expressive painting	7hr	H JP	NR	N Rayan
11/7/2017 8:50 - 3:30 .	- Own painting lesson did it. art (parent diary expressive) aiding work. indicated children - IBC - numeracy work	7hr	H	NR	N Rayan
12/07/2017 8:50 - 4:00	- Art Room - Games (cheer) - ethics office work.	8hr	H	NR	N Rayan

Appendix 13

20/7/17 8:50 - 3:30	Paxus, films Classroom work	7hr	*(signature)*	NR	NRo
21/7/17 8:50 - 3:30	Cleaning filing faxing Ethics - Hang procedure	7hr	*(signature)*	NR	N Rogers
24/7/17 9:05 - 2:10	- Ethics Paper work , ensuring all files up to date leaflet correspondence	6hr	*(signature)*	NR	N Rogers
25/7/17 8:45 - 02:11	Paper work, leyen court kids dinner kluty Nurture.	6hr	*(signature)*	NR	N Rogers

140 HOURS + 25 MINS.

Appendix 14

Family structure and criminality; A literature review.

Acknowledgements

An immense amount of time, organisation, determination and willingness went into the creation of this dissertation. Whilst on this written journey of completing my dissertation there are a few individuals who have made the completion of this dissertation possible. First and foremost, I would like to thank my supervisor, Dr Elizabeth Yardley, for showing me the ins and outs of writing a dissertation piece, in terms of structure, content, and forming a proposal which was manageable, doable, contemporary and academical. I would also like to thank my supervisor for taking the time to respond to my e-mails and being available for meetings when requested. As well as my supervisor, I would like to thank my mother, Gulnaz Begum, for ensuring I was always on task when doing my work at home. Finally, I would like to thank my fiancé, Shahir Rehman, and

course peer Sadia Jehan Khattak for motivating me to get my work done and ensuring my work made sense.

Abstract

To demonstrate to readers the possible relationship between family structure and criminality it is important for readers to understand the concept of key terms, explore key themes and understand key theoretical backgrounds of previous research that has been provided for family structure, relatable subjects and criminality. This report is to inform readers on literature that has already been produced in regard to the criminological discipline of the family structure and criminality. This report shall inform readers by exploring through a range of themes that can be found throughout the literature that is being examined. The themes to be explored range from a biological perspective, for example, the inheritable criminal gene, to a more social perspective, for example, the abusive family. As well as the investigative procedure for the literature review, information gained regarding the themes explored and an overview of all the materials that have been collected throughout the investigative procedure shall be discussed in a descriptive, analytical and critiquing section of the dissertation.

Introduction

A 2012 Ministry of Justice report conducted by Williams, et al (2012) showing childhood and family backgrounds of prisoners concluded that issues arising for prisoners during their childhood, such as family issues and educative issues, had contributed to their actions completed as an adult (Williams, et al, 2012). The maltreatment of prisoners which resulted in their behavioural changes included sexual, physical, and mental abuse during their childhood (Williams, et al, 2012). The report also concluded that the structures of the families also varied and contributed to some of their behaviourisms today (Williams, et al, 2012).

Questions over what 'makes' an offender should be one of the most central considerations for contemporary criminology (Loughran, et al, 2016). However, the neoliberal focus upon the sovereign individual and the concept of personal responsibility has led to the dominance of the rational choice model (Boudon, 2003). Which suggests that individuals indulge in criminal activities due to their own autonomous, independent decision making and choices (Boudon, 2003). The rational choice model exercises the belief that all individuals are fully in control of their own behaviours, therefore, the criminality is considered to be the result of individual decisions (Boudon, 2003). It is assumed that all are equally rational, due to the exclusive onus on personal responsibility (Boudon, 2003).

The rational choice model lacks the acknowledgement of external factors such as the economy, education and culture, that can contribute to one becoming a criminal, which are also ignored within the context of the contemporary criminal justice system (Loughran, et al, 2016). In relation to the theory's ignorance of external factors, many procedures that aim to increase the rehabilitative rates of an individual are decreased (Loughran, 2016). The ability to produce efficient crime prevention methods are also decreased again due to lack of acknowledgement of the contributions the external factors may cause alongside the personal causations of one becoming a criminal (Loughran, et al, 2016). In relation to the issues that can be caused by not acknowledging external factors, such as the decrease of efficacy of rehabilitative and crime prevention methods, the denial of the factors in essence brings to light the fact that we need to incorporate both external and internal factors to one becoming a criminal, in order to produce viable procedures and tactics that can be used to prevent crime and exercise rehabilitative practices within an individual (Loughran, et al, 2016). One particular social institution that is important in shaping an individual is the family (Eriksson, et al, 2015). There is literature surrounding the role of the family in regard to the making of an offender, which this essay will examine.

The aim of this research piece is to gain insight into the relationship between family structures and criminality. It does so by examining the existing literature in relation to three key themes: the inheritable criminal gene, the abusive family, and birth order. In the next section, the key research questions will be outlined.

Research Question

'Is there a relationship between family structures and criminality?' The question aims to provide an in-depth but broader understanding of the discipline and how it can affect criminal behaviours.

Research Aims

- To understand the connection between family structures and criminality.

- To explore whether family structures alone can affect criminal behaviour.

- To discuss the different sub-disciplines that can be created under the family structure.

- To discuss the issues with previous research in the understanding of family structures, respected themes and criminality.

Methodological Approach

This literature review shall be formed by using a qualitative secondary data method in which existing literature shall be cross-examined in order to find relevant themes, which will then create a discussion and conclusion on the overall findings of the literature (Caulfield and Hill, 2014). This method aids the researcher in pinpointing any themes and allows a more in-depth analysis of research already produced (Caulfield and Hill, 2014).

An epistemological approach for a qualitative research-based question would be interpretivism (Bryman, 2016). Interpretivism can be used to make sense of the social world (Bryman, 2016). It interprets data to make sense of a social world, whereas other theories may look towards more natural scientific reasonings (Bryman, 2016). It allows the researcher to find, extract, critique and define the research area in question (Bryman, 2016).

The data analysis method that is going to be used for a secondary research type as such is the thematic data analysis method (Braun and Clarke, 2006). The aim of a thematic analysis method is to locate themes, pinpoint or examine data (Braun and Clarke, 2006). As mentioned above, this method allows the researcher to combine a number of previous literature and critiques, summaries and link different sources (Braun and Clarke, 2006). This is done to review the literature on a topic, make recommendations or to connect your research question and the literature findings together (Braun and Clarke, 2006).

Ethical Considerations

In order to prevent ethical jeopardies, this research piece has been approved by the Birmingham City Universities Ethics

Board (Birmingham City University, 2006). In accordance with this to promote and support good practice the ethical guidelines produced via the British Society of Criminology shall be maintained throughout the piece (British Society of Criminology, 2015). As this is a secondary research piece, one should take into consideration that any information used should be properly referenced in-text and as a bibliography or reference list (British Society of Criminology, 2015). One should reference abiding by the referencing system used by the respected society's body – an example of a referencing system is the Harvard referencing style (British Society of Criminology, 2015). In addition to this, when referencing sometimes citations of other literature are included and also online publication dates may differ from the actual written date; the researcher should take this into account when providing the appropriate reference as this may lead to penalisation under plagiarism (British Society of Criminology, 2015). Finally, as this research piece is potentially searching for information that some may find distressing, the researcher is familiarised with the counselling team at the university that can provide support, and as well as this the researcher's supervisor is on hand to assist with enquires and issues (Birmingham City University, 2006).

Themes

Previous literature on the topic of criminality and family structure focuses upon the individual's childhood as a means to differentiate the individual from the standard social construct that describes how a 'normal' individual should behave and how their life should be like (UKEssays, 2018). Previous literature concentrates less upon the causes of crime or the connection to crime and more upon the individual and their circumstances (UKEssays, 2018). Therefore, in respect of the research's questions and aims, this literature review shall focus upon three key themes. These themes will allow us to delve into the question of whether there is a relatability between family structures and criminality, and as a result, these three key themes that have been chosen will also allow us to give an in-depth response to the question we aim to answer. We shall start off by first looking at genes and criminality, in which the inheritable criminal gene 'MAOA' shall be examined. This will be followed by studies exploring the role of birth order and criminality. Lastly, we shall examine the research that has been produced on the role of familial abuse in regard to criminality.

The Inheritable Criminal Gene

Graves (2013) explains that biological determinism suggests that there is a relationship between genetic structure and social position (Graves, 2013). Graves (2013) claims that, specifically, biological determinism has made claims about groups of people, especially the socially subordinated (including racial/ethnic minorities, women and gays), suggesting that their disadvantages do not result from social structure, but instead that the social structure results from the inherited superior attributes of the socially advantaged versus the inherited inferiorities of the socially subordinate (Graves, 2013). Graves (2013) further explains the ideology of biological determinism by explaining the theoretical frameworks and research findings of a twentieth-century biologist known as Stephen Jay Gould (1941-2002) (Graves, 2013).

Graves (2013) explains that Gould's work on biological determinism suggests that biological determinism holds and shares behavioural norms and the social and economic differences between human groups, primarily races, classes, and sexes, arise from inherited inborn distinctions; and society, in this sense, is an accurate reflection of biology (Graves, 2013). He goes on to further explain that the idea of biological determinism is somewhat ancient – in the western world going back to at least the Platonic Greeks. Biological determinism is inherent in the thinking of Plato's student Aristotle's concept of the scale of nature (Graves, 2013). Aristotle's scale of nature was an attempt to create a hierarchical classification of the living (and supernatural) in the scheme of Greek cosmology (earth, water, air and fire) (Graves, 2013). Earthier animals, such as worms and other invertebrates, occupied the lowest rungs on his ladder, followed by more 'fiery' animals, humans, demigods, and the gods (Graves, 2013). Within humans, there were scales as well, with some born to be slaves whereas others were born to be rulers (Graves, 2013).

Graves' thesis on biological determinism and its relation to social positions explains that characteristics of genetics and traits can be carried through bloodlines and whilst this may hold some truth, this does not explain criminal behaviourisms present in individuals. Raine (2008) explains that whilst families can share genetics and social dispositions based on those characteristics, that does not mean that each individual born into those surroundings will have the same experiences, thoughts, effects on their own personal, social and others' lives (Raine, 2008). As well as this, the researches' commitment to specify the disadvantages faced by those who are subservient to the dominant classes concentrates most of its findings and conclusions based on biased opinions that social dispositions and negative attributes are faced only by those belonging to subservient classes and that those of dominant classes do not have characteristics that are defined as negative or criminal in the realm of social structure or society itself. Therefore, to solely blame genetics on criminality via the idea of biological determinism can be both treacherous and deceiving; as though bloodlines can share genes that are known as criminal genes, there should also be the addition of a deep social culture that is drilled into the minds of family members since they are born, which as mentioned by Raine (2008) in essence is also a causation to families becoming criminal and holds more cues to the causation of criminal families such as the mafia families becoming what they are, better than just the reliance on the inheritable gene (Raine, 2008). As well as this, the issue of solely blaming genetics for criminals' behaviour can also affect judiciary practices as the inheritance of a gene that is out of one's control can be classed as a medical illness and, therefore, can cause altercations in sentences and in some cases to justify the crimes people commit, and render cases free of charge under many mental pleas (Raine, 2008).

When looking at the concept of biological determinism under the idea of family structure and criminality, many other factors to one's journey of life are ignored. Individuals may share genetics; however, they will not share the same mental thought processes, social environments outside the home environment, or personal non-familial experiences. It may be that these external experiences are what differentiate individuals from each other and thus the idea of just basing causes to criminalisation on science and the body is similar to that of the rational choice model. As, although both have different concepts, they both exclude factors that are external to their beliefs, making their theories single-minded and open to reform.

In relation to the inheritable criminal gene 'MAOA', Wilson (2002) explains that although criminals share a common genetic flaw and it can be easily said that this is what determines their criminal abilities, it is indeed much more complex than just that (Wilson, 2002). He goes on to further explain that human behaviour begins in the brain, every decision we make is based upon small spaces that separate the 100 billion nerve cells in the human brain (Wilson, 2002). Contrary to appearances, neurons, as brain cells are called, do not physically touch like wires (Wilson, 2002). They are separated by tiny gaps known as synapses (Wilson, 2002). To communicate across the void, a nerve cell releases a tiny amount of a class of compounds known as neurotransmitters (Wilson,

2002). Wilson (2002) suggests that the left-over neurotransmitters can open the door to understanding how genes can influence criminal behaviours (Wilson, 2002). Wilson's (2002) article also suggests that during a research study enabled by the University of Wisconsin, the psychologist frequently found that violent inmates have been abused as children (Wilson, 2002). Yet a history of abuse by itself is not a predictor of future criminal behaviour (Wilson, 2002). One obvious possibility was that the two factors associated with criminality, genes and abuse, were somehow related (Wilson, 2002).

Wilson's proposition on inheritable criminal genes shows not only that there is a possibility that genes can hold a connection to criminalisation, but Wilson's article also shows that other factors are necessary for the causation of criminalisation. The presence and acknowledgement of external factors outside the body, for example childhood experiences and most importantly individual experiences, shows the concurrent necessities that whilst genes, more importantly, neurons may play an important role in the formation of individuals becoming criminalised, this cannot be the only factor; external factors such as the environment, individual responses, social opportunities and the individual's own choices can and need to be present in order for an individual to become criminalised within the social, psychological and academical contexts (Raine, 2013).

In relation to family structure and criminality, the criminal gene MAOA suggests that families that hold certain gene characteristics or lack certain genetic abilities can be born criminal and as a result may be predominantly criminal within later years of their life (Raine, 2013). However, with that being said, as Wilson mentions, you cannot solely blame genes and the lack of natural behavioural characteristics on an individual becoming a criminal (Wilson, 2002). You also cannot socially or psychologically blame a family for the offspring becoming criminal due to their genetical DNA; it is indeed noted and necessary that external factors contribute to an individual showcasing such behaviours that are seen as criminal (Raine, 2013). With that being said, this suggestion of the necessity of external factors in the making of a criminal upholds the debate surrounding nature and nurture and defuses the reliance that genes can hold memory cues to an individual becoming criminalised and, therefore, it is seen as a secondary theory in the academical realm (Raine, 2013).

Another point to take into consideration when discussing the ideology surrounding the idea of criminal genes and criminality is that individuals are not born criminals. They can be taught to be criminal and, therefore, to the social world it may be presented as being born criminal; this is due to cultural, social, parental or environmental influences being instilled into the individual's mind frame from a young age. However, there is also the idea that it is ultimately the individual's choice on whether they act upon the information that has been fed to them (Clarke and Felson, 2017). This idea is even viable if the individual was taught this from a young age, it is still the individual's choice on whether or not they wish to act as the chosen term they are being labelled as (Clarke and Felson, 2017). The theory that upholds this belief is the dominant theory of the criminological realm that understands criminals and is known as the rational choice model (Clarke and Felson, 2017). The rational choice model exercises the belief that individuals choose the pathway to criminality on their own, it is their autonomous choice to follow their desires of becoming criminalised (Clarke and Felson, 2017). This deflects the idea that individuals are born criminal or have subdued to criminal behaviourisms due to their environment or upbringing (Clarke and Felson, 2017). Instead, it focuses upon the idea of the individual themselves and gives personal responsibility towards criminalisation rather than external factors, which although is a problem within itself, shows that there are more precedence and a common belief that individuals commit crimes due to their own rational choice (Clarke and Felson, 2017). This is prevalent as it is the dominant theory when it comes to discussing the causation of criminals becoming criminalised (Clarke and Felson, 2017).

Birth Order

A theory that can be used to explain birth order and criminality is Alfred Adler's birth order theory. Adler's theory suggests that birth order, in other words, the order of the children in a family, affects a child's personality (Gustafson, 2010). For example, a first-born child is given more attention, this child is less depressed, more powerful towards the other siblings as this child is the oldest and is closer to being their second parent; as well as this, this child is also known to have less or no delinquent issues (Gustafson, 2010). The youngest child of the family is flaunted with goods and attention; this is due to their older sibling moving on to different emotional and personality stages; this child is thought to be less delinquent but also may hold some delinquency due to the leniency shown by parents when the child exhibits bad behaviours (Gustafson, 2010). Finally, middle children, middle children of the family, often share attention but also gain somewhat less than the older and baby sibling; this child is thought to exhibit the most delinquent behaviours; as well as this they may also exhibit mental health issues (Gustafson, 2010).

In terms of family structure and criminality, the birth order theory often draws upon the issue faced by the middle children of families, which from a theoretical outlook is often referred to as a middle-child syndrome (Kotin, 1995). The theory suggests that middle children are more prone to becoming delinquent children as they are classed as children who have less attention from their parents (Kotin, 1995). This attention is most craved by children, as it signifies love, identity and need from a child's point of view (Kotin, 1995). The middle child also has to fight for identity and a position within the household against their other siblings; again this competition is viewed and fought out from the middle child's family position stance only (Kotin, 1995). Due to the lack of attention and constant fighting for attention, the middle child is believed to encounter an identity crisis from childhood to adulthood which through the years can accelerate and as a result the individual may become depressed or mentally unstable and as a way to release their issues they involve themselves with delinquent behaviourisms as a method to not only self-preserve but to find purpose, to identify with others alike (Kotin, 1995). This is because they class themselves as outcasts and aim to band together with other delinquents alike in a bid to find family, aim, purpose, and most of all, an identity (Kotin, 1995).

The effects of birth order are most prominent within middle-children of the family. This is not only suggested by Adler's birth order theory, but research produced on children and delinquency also comments on this during conclusions and research outcomes. For example, Roche and Begue (2005) suggest that birth order alongside differential parental control assisted in middle children of the family engaging in minor offences and some serious offences more than their firstborn siblings (Rocher and Begue, 2005). The French research piece suggests this is partially due to the firstborn being more supervised by the parents or guardians than the middle child (Roche and Begue, 2005). Roche and Begue (2005) also suggest that although birth order and parental control may affect middle-children in regard to crime on a more delinquent level rather than serious offence crimes (Roche and Begue, 2005). Nonetheless this research piece conducted by Roche and Begue (2005) suggests that birth order position plays a moderate part role in delinquent behaviour and that the birth order effect is partially induced by differential parental control (Roche and Begue, 2005).

However, with this being said, there is still the argument of whether the term middle-child syndrome actually exists; this is due to the lack of the phrase being used. As well as this critique, there is also a conclusion of whether birth order can realistically only affect middle children – could this phenomena branch out to the youngest of the siblings also? This is suggested as primary research studies, for example from Davidson (2016), show the youngest child also exhibits similar behavioural traits to that of a middle-child (Davidson, 2016). In addition to this point, the idea surrounded around birth order and delinquency is that the middle-child has an absence within the household that the child believes can be filled within other social realms, and may find themselves drawn towards delinquent societies as they are the most welcoming when it comes to outcasts (Davidson, 2016). The addition of the youngest child also exhibiting these behaviours and moving towards delinquency can also be incorporated within this idea; however, research also shows that unlike middle-children, the youngest child, when manifesting delinquent behaviours, is promoted with love, affection, and becomes more noticeable within the household, therefore delinquent behaviours can resolve on their own over time, whereas for the middle-child the noticeable behavioural changes presented by the child are often misread by parents and thus the effects caused by the void of love in the first place are presented more within the middle child of the family more than the youngest, which as a result leads a middle-child towards a more delinquent life overall compared to the youngest and oldest siblings (Davidson, 2016). In light of all this information, it is still too biased to say that it is only middle children that elicit this kind of behaviour, as there has not been enough research produced to counter such conclusions (Davidson, 2016).

Another theory that can be used to explain birth order and criminality is Karl Marx's 18th-century conflict theory. Karl Marx's conflict theory suggests that life is like a competition similar to that of Darwin's survival of the fittest theory (Jones, 2007). Marx suggested that seeing as life is like a competition, the main focus on individuals' lives are: distribution of materialistic, social and mental gains which incorporates sustainability, power, inequality and resourcefulness (Jones, 2007). Jones (2007) further explains that conflict theory best explains predominant and powerful social changes, but Marx's theory can also be fitting within the family realm of social disciplines, in terms of family interactions, structures and more (Jones, 2007).

In terms of family structure and delinquency, Marx's theory suggests that family structure may reinforce some kind of competition of usefulness at home between siblings, and therefore bring about different emotive and physical behaviours in order to achieve this usefulness (Jones, 2007). Marx suggests those children that cannot reach their usefulness potential at home often sought other areas outside of the home to find their personal usefulness – in Marx's theory it suggests this personal usefulness they earn outside the family home is there to make-up for the usefulness they cannot find at home and acts as a half winner kind of deal in terms of the competition for usefulness (Jones, 2007).

Although the theory of conflict grasps the concept of family structure well, there are some things that are in need of further clarification. For example, the theory suggests that children who have siblings involve themselves with some sort of competition in order to find and stay useful within the family environment; as well as this 'the family' is seen as a staple icon that is incorporated into many aspects of life and is seen as a fundamental bond within socialising and psychological realms; this then suggests that 'the family' is one of the main focuses of individuals' lives which will aid them in gaining power, sustainability, inequality and resourcefulness, and this theory also insinuates that having a limited family or a non-bonded family reduces your ability to achieve this (Merryweather, 2017). However, this theory does not specifically state how necessary a family is for an individual's search for power and sustainability, and therefore limits our knowledge (Merryweather, 2017). This is due to the main fact that this theory has not given an idea or definition or structure of the term 'family' (Merryweather, 2017). As a result of the lack of definition of a family or idea of a general structure of a family, there are questions as to whether this theory abides by all types of family structures, as socially some family types are seen as disadvantageous compared to others (Merryweather, 2017).

In addition to the theories already used to explain birth order and criminality, we can use another theory, the labelling theory, which can be used to facilitate an understanding of the need for the middle children of families to comply to criminal or anti-social behaviours. In 1963, Becker suggested that individuals may self-identify themselves with certain cultures, words and thoughts, and that society itself has socially constructed definitions of the terms or ideas that these individuals have self-identified themselves with (Cullen and Wilcox, 2010). These identities that individuals take on are quite often based on the definitions of the terms or thoughts issued by society, and based on these definitions that are issued, Becker believes that the individual will behave and socially abide by the norms given to that definition (Cullen and Wilcox, 2010). Becker believes the individual's characteristics will always portray the definition created by society, whether that be a negative definition or a positive one (Cullen and Wilcox, 2010). In addition to the labelling theory, two traits that are often associated with the theory is the self-fulling prophecy, which is the idea that one commits to the ideas or identities society associates with them until they are clearly and truly identifiable with those certain characteristics; and the other trait which is usually associated with labelling theory is stereotyping: stereotyping is a widely recognisable associate of definitions, thoughts or words surrounding a certain type of person or thing, often stereotyping is common with negative labelling (Cullen and Wilcox, 2010).

In terms of family structure, labelling theory suggests that the family is a staple societal norm and belonging to a compliant, normal, law-abiding family is an identifiable characteristic that is taught and spread throughout educative years from ages as low as four (Cullen and Wilcox, 2010). As the family is an identifiable characteristic to a greater society, not belonging to one or belonging to one you are unidentifiable with, may clash with personas and give some individuals the feeling to rebel or seek societies that they feel they belong in; sometimes these societies they find themselves belonging to, for example a throw-away society, is looked down on by greater society, and thus individuals find themselves outcasts from a greater society which in turn may lead to some complying in negative and delinquent behaviour (Cullen and Wilcox, 2010).

In regard to child delinquency and labelling theory, often it is believed that it is middle children of the families that rebel and can show strands of delinquency (Bernburg, et al, 2006). This is mainly due to the fact that middle children, as suggested by other theories like birth order and coercion theory, believe they have no real purpose within the normative staple family environment, and thus are believed to be the most common sibling or child type to rebel, which in return offers them a negative label to live by as they often include themselves with societies that are degraded by society (Bernburg, et al, 2006). A term often associated with middle children during research produced on children and family structure is middle-child syndrome (Bernburg, et al, 2006). Middle-child syndrome is the belief of non-existence from a child's stance within a family structure of multiple children (Bernburg, et al, 2006). However, within this theory and its commentaries, there is still a question of whether or not the term middle-child syndrome actually exists and thus whether the idea of middle children having negative behavioural traits is also questionable. This is because research conducted by Gates, et al, (1988) shows that middle children, as well as the youngest sibling, can show negative behavioural traits within family environments, identifying that it is not just middle children that face these issues whilst growing up.

To further represent the point of middle children and their psychological position on identity and labelling, we can further use the work of Gates, et al (1988). Gates produced research that suggests first-born children were less likely to be expected to fall into depressive states and contract anxiety. The study was constructed on children aged between 7-12 years old who were given three different tests, which are as follows: children's depression inventory, state-trait anxiety inventory for children and Piers-Harris self-concept scale (Gates, et al, 1988). The test showed that first-born children showed fewer signs of anxiety and depression compared to their middle and youngest siblings (Gates, et al, 1988). It also showed that girls were more prone to depressive states and anxiety than their male counterparts (Gates, et al, 1988). Although research shows a concentration towards middle children and their vulnerability to criminality, research produced by Gates (1988), Roche and Begue (2003) opens mindful questions surrounding the existence of the term middle-child syndrome, but also whether the issue of identifying to a positive label can be a path for all children to undergo and that the likes of middle children or any child can also take naturally and socially longer to find this positively labelled identity than other individuals.

Another point to take into consideration when discussing birth order and criminality is the reliability and helpfulness of the research itself. Nystul (1976) suggests that research produced around birth order and psychological traits has been confused due to independent variables (Nystul, 1976). This is because research studying the same concept shows two outcomes: one which shows a relationship between psychological traits and birth order, and one which shows no relationship at all (Nystul, 1976). Nystul (1976) further explains that research produced by Schooler (1972) suggests that these confusions may be decreased if one looks at other dependent variables, for example, the sex of the children and density of the children, which will allow future researchers to look towards more consistent patterns within their own research pieces (Nystul, 1976).

The Abusive Family

The final theme that will be examined and researched is the abusive family. To represent the connections between the abusive family, family structures and criminality we can use a range of theories. We can use the theory of social control. Hirschi's 1969 social control theory explains that individuals intertwine together via a social bond, the social bond constitutes from four elementswhich are as follows: attachment to other individuals, commitment to following rules, community involvement through typical acceptable behaviours, and a basic value system (Morris, et al, 2011). Hirschi goes on to further explain that individuals who break the law or interact in anti-social behaviours do so due to the individual's societal bonds breaking (Morris, et al, 2011). The individual's societal bonds breaking can be due to the lack of abundance or disinterest of one or more of the four elements of a societal bond (Morris, et al, 2011).

In terms of family structure, Hirschi's social control theory suggests that the bond between a child and parent is intertwined immensely within these four elements of social bonding, in particular, attachment to others and a basic value system (Morris, et al, 2011). Therefore, if a bond between the parent and child is understood by the child to be broken, the child may refrain from the society they class themselves with as a method of grievances, but also to heal and re-emerge into another society in a bid to self-identify (Morris, et al, 2011). The grievances and need for self-identity and belonging are a suggestive cause to delinquent behaviour in children and the causes of criminality within adults (Morris, et al, 2011).

To further explain the social bonding described within the social control theory, we can look at research conducted by Williams (2012). Within Williams' research the generic family structure was broken down into the many types there are such as a two-parent, single parent, foster family, and adoptive families, and was examined on the basis of the following: upbringing, family neglection and behavioural learning from other family members (Williams, et al, 2012). The finding of this part of the investigation found many prisoners came from neglectful backgrounds and foster homes, and also had family members who had been convicted of low-level crimes, which for some resulted in imprisonment; there was also many cases of domestic violence upon themselves or loved ones (Williams, et al, 2012).

Hirschi and Williams' work both represent social control theory and suggests that a child and parent share such a bond, which can be believed to be so intertwining to such an extent that it is as if behaviourisms and social norms are copied through parent to child. This point can be further exemplified through the work of Marono (2018) and Navarro (2018). Marono (2018) and Navarro's (2018) research piece, which aimed to explain how different types of child abuse can be used to profile serial offenders, concludes that amongst the 50 serial offenders they had examined, a past of child abuse was at a higher percentage than it would be if the general public was examined (TheBritishPsychologicalSociety, 2018). Alongside this, Marono (2018) and Navarro (2018) discovered that the type of serial offender matched with the type of child abuse they received (TheBritishPsychologicalSociety, 2018). For example, a serial offender who had encountered acts of sexual abuse as a child was more prone to being connected to anger, lust/love typology of a serial offender (TheBritishPsychologicalSociety, 2018). This offender type also has a tendency to overkill, post-mortem sex, and the movement of the body from a different place of the murder (TheBritishPsychologicalSociety, 2018). Marono (2018) and Navarro (2018) also suggested that parents who abuse their children, physically as well as psychologically, instil in them the almost instinctive reliance upon violence as a first resort to any challenge (TheBritishPsychologicalSociety, 2018).

However, with that being said, there are arguments, for example suggested by Ferguson, et al (2010), that suggest children see the world through their own eyes and may also have social bonds similar to that of parental bonds with other individuals (Ferguson, et al, 2010). Therefore, these extra social bonds could also be the make or break reason for child delinquency (Ferguson, et al, 2010). This argument can be further actualised by looking at child interactions with gangs and gang members (Ferguson, et al, 2010). These bonds created by gang members can be so mentally holding that one may act out in order to voice their treatment, thus showcasing themselves as delinquent behaviours (Ferguson, et al, 2010). As well as this, not only in a negative light but also a positive light, there are many more social bonds a child views other than a parental bond that may hold significance to a child's life and understanding of life – these may come in the form of educative, blood, social or romantic bonds (Ferguson, et al, 2010).

Another theory can represent the discipline of family abuse in the context of criminality is Patterson's 1982 coercion theory. The coercion theory explores the idea of reinforcement. Patterson explains that the relationship between a parent and child can be seen as a mutual reinforcement in which parents inadvertently reinforce the child's difficult behaviour, which in turn legitimises the adult's behaviour in the children's eye (Colvin, et al, 2002). This process of a child's difficult behaviour and legitimisation of an adult's behaviour occurs like an ongoing cycle where the parent and child take turns to reinforce the negative attitudes they create until one, either parent or child, wins (Colvin, et al, 2002).

Within the context of family structure, coercion theory suggests, if a child watches a parent behave in a manner they dislike just to get what the parent wants from the child, the child deems this behaviour acceptable for future social encounters they may bump into (Colvin, et al, 2002). Thus, when they are older or become of an age where they can exhibit their emotions and actions from a socially interactive level, their behaviour reflects that of their parents (Colvin, et al, 2002). Furthermore, based on the type of behaviours the parent exhibits, the behaviour is seen as a negative from society, may be marked as delinquent and may also act as a cause for delinquent behaviours to rise (Colvin, et al, 2002). This is most common in cases where children are singled out or have social interaction issues such as anxiety, depression, psychosis or autism (Colvin, et al, 2002).

This point can be further exemplified within the work of Cuadra (2014), Cuadra, et al (2014) suggests that although not all individuals who have received maltreatment during their childhood are likely to become criminalised in adulthood, there is a small percentage that does and it is for this percentage that conduction of research as such is most important (Cuadra, et al, 2014). Cuadra, et al (2014) goes on to state that a study conducted by McGrath, et al (2011) shows a social learning perspective within the frequent outcome of maltreated children and criminalisation during their adulthood (Cuadra, et al, 2014). The theories proposed by McGarth, et al (2011) suggest that individuals who are exposed to direct or indirect violence or abusive experiences, which can range from sexual to physical to mental, within their early developmental stages, are more like to adopt corresponding attitudes and beliefs emphasizing the reinforcing qualities of violence, and engage in offensive or abusive behaviours later on in life (Cuadra, et al, 2014). Cuadra, et al (2014) gives further insight, by suggesting that a key element to this cycle of violence is that victims internalize maladaptive, violence-support beliefs and attitudes, including that physical aggression is acceptable and a useful way to accomplish personal and interpersonal goals such as managing stress or resolving conflicts, and thus, model abusive behaviours in relating with others (Cuadra, et al, 2014).

Coercion theory holds a similar manifesto with social control theory, in regards to the purpose and social creational methods a parental or guardian figure holds for a child. However, as mentioned with social control theory, arguments show that children make sense and see the world through their own eyes, and therefore, other relations or incidences outside the control of parental or guardian bonding or social learning acts can contribute to a child's delinquent behaviour (Snyder and Merritt, 2014). These social encounters, which are separate from those given by a parental or guardian figure, can hold precedence over the social reinforcement methods it is believed parents or guardians hold against their child (Snyder and Merritt, 2014). Therefore, to ultimately blame parents solely for the delinquent behaviourisms a child may produce or abide by is inadequate (Snyder and Merritt, 2014). As well as this, giving sole responsibility to a parental or guardian figure on how a child is raised and what they learn, can dismiss any other forms of social learning they may encounter which had held back research as well understanding of a child and delinquency, which may cause further delinquency in children to rise and may mean that reform services and appropriate reformative suggestions are kept at a low/minimal (Synder and Merritt, 2014).

To further exemplify the methods a child may use to socially interact with the environment they reside in, and that is outside the control of the parental and guardian's realm is at school or through online services. Studies from both Ferguson, et al (2010) and Perren, et al (2006) show violent video games not solely but in conjunction with various other environmental factors contributed to the violent outburst and delinquent behaviour present in young individuals of the 8th grade which are usually around the age of

12-14. During their research, the idea surrounding bullying was also examined, which both found different conclusions. Ferguson, et al (2010) found that bullying and delinquent behaviourisms were predicted by the child's trait aggressions and stress levels (Ferguson, et al, 2010). Parental involvement was subservient to the causes of this stress and bullying behaviourisms (Ferguson, et al, 2010). Whereas, Perren, et al (2006) found that bullies and bullying victims were also perpetrators and victims of violence delinquency, as well as this, the level of delinquency differed in the different sexes and education types (Perren, et al, 2006). Perren, et al (2006) also found that pupils who were bullied reported lower peer acceptance than bullies and non-involved pupils (Perren, et al, 2006). Bullies, as well as perpetrators and victims of violence delinquency, reported lower family support than non-involved adolescents (Perren, et al, 2006).

Both Ferguson (2010) and Perren's (2006) work shows social interactions that individuals face outside the parental social nurturing realm can influence one's social learning curve to such an extent that they may show delinquent behaviourisms and later become criminalised; however, both of their works also suggest that although parental involvement is minimal within the social realm of teenagers, parental social interactions can still be a factor that affects one's behaviour. So, to blame the effects of social interactions on the latter is improper as any social interaction can persuade an individual to become delinquent; therefore, to suggest criminalisation is caused by either is wrong as it can be anything in a individual's life that can cause criminalisation; yes, collectively there may be some common factors of parental issues, bullying, video games and more, but this is not based on individual circumstances, it is based on conclusions from research based on the masses (Merryweather, 2017).

Discussion and Conclusion

Looking at the information retrieved from the articles used within this essay, we have found a few key points. The first is that although we have three separate themes, they are interlinking in terms of their rationale for family structures and criminality. For example, although the inheritable criminal gene and abusive family may be seen as different, the essence of a family trait and family characteristics being shared are the same in regard to the influence of the idea on a individual's psychological and sociological nature. The idea that a criminal gene, family characteristic, the behaviour of family members can be taught or shared amongst offspring and others who reside within this family is something which is proposed both within the academia surrounding the abusive family and the inheritable criminal genes theme. As well as this, all the themes share a common debatable critique of nature vs nurture (Johnson, 1986). Looking at the criminal gene, birth order and the abusive family, we can see that although they are of either side, the criminal gene being the nature and abusive family and birth order being nurture, the counterargument for each is the opposite. The idea that we are either sociologically/psychologically impaired or biologically inadaptable is something that runs throughout the academia found for all of the themes (Johnson,

1986). Which as a result limits the research in rooting probable causes for the causations of criminalisation within individuals, as the research dwells more on the individual's acts and lifestyle like a story, rather than using it to distinguish or propose probable causes to individuals becoming criminalised.

A second point is that the themes lack the ability to understand and incorporate the attendance of external relations in an individual's life. The relationship between the themes and criminality is examined, yes; however, the lack of responsibility placed upon external relations outside of the family suggest that families hold precedence in an individual's life, more than any other type of relationship, which is a false representation on not only family relations but an individual's social bonding methods and the mental and social influences individuals who are not related can hold on each other (Boccio and Beaver, 2017). Friendship, work, love and subconscious bonding are seen as secondary influences within an individual's life, which creates a social construct that an individual needs a family to be complete and not just any family but one that is represented and created by a societal realm of individuals that are seen as dominant within the status of human beings (Boccio and Beaver, 2017). The magnification of a set vision on what a family should look like, and the repercussions this may have on other relationship types as well as individuals' mental states if these normal family standards are not met, is something which is hardly examined or spoken of (Boccio and Beaver, 2017). A prime example of a sub-theme that excludes external relationships and promotes the need for a family structure that is socially constructed is middle child syndrome. Middle children are seen as the children who are most likely to become criminalised due to the lack of their need in their family home. Their purpose within their family is measured by themselves. The academia around middle children and birth order signifies that children are wary of their status within their families and not having one may cause delinquent or criminal behaviourisms within later years of life. However, the access and support of external relations to an individual are rarely discussed, thus leaving out suggestions to promote good behaviour but also suggestions on how one may not become a criminal or delinquent due to external relations.

A third point to be made is that the themes excuse the most dominant theory in the criminological realm that exemplifies the individuals' individual causation to becoming criminalised. The dominant theory being the rational choice model. Yes, individuals can become criminalised through issues surrounding their family structure and, therefore, can be influenced within their decision to becoming criminalised, as some things in their lives are not as up to scratch as they should be and this may default their mental thought process to become negative; however, ultimately it is their decision to become criminalised (Parks, 2013). Even within the context of the criminal gene, genes and dominant characteristics can be shown, yes, but it is the individual who needs to learn to control, change or defuse the issue they are faced with (Parks, 2013). Which in essence still leads an individual to choose to become criminalised. This is something that is not mentioned as much. The focus on subservient models that can reflect upon an individual's criminalisation is good and necessary;

however, ignoring or excluding the dominant model should not be a priority (Parks, 2013). As well as this, academia surrounding the themes have shown that individuals have a desire to choose the criminal or delinquent lifestyle that they present themselves with and thus, this may suggest that rational choice, alongside family structures, can influence criminalisation (Parks, 2013). Although all the themes exemplify the role that rational choice may play within a family structural and criminalisation process and context, we shall use the abusive family as an example; the abusive family general academic profile is that individuals socially learn and copycat characteristics from their families, especially in regards to negative behaviours (Parks, 2013). However, the initial thought to copycat or socially learn these behaviours are not socially or mentally applied, it is a choice. Manipulation is unspoken of through these academic abilities; therefore, it is surely the choice of the individual to learn and act out what they see from their surroundings (Parks, 2013). The implication of rational choice in conjunction with abusive families is something which is disregarded. This could be in a bid to exclude the dominant theory and highlight subservient theories, but it could be an aspect that is possibly less explored.

A final point that can be drawn from the academia investigated is that throughout all of these themes, family structure is still a key role player in the understanding of how the themes play their roles within a criminal context. Throughout the literature found for criminal genes, birth order and abusive families, although the literature examined is aimed at the individual theme, they all propose the necessity and purpose for a family structure to be present in order for their theories and suggestions to work and make sense (Wright, 2017). However, with that said, there are a few things that are not mentioned regarding family structures. The first is what the generic family structure looks like on which they are basing their conclusions and suggestions, the second is conclusions are based on the generic individual rather the different types of family members, and the third is that the family which is being spoken of has no disadvantages, it is suggesting that this is an idea of social mechanisms that are needed within our lives and due to not having the generic structural one which is also not described; these themes can be produced in which criminalisation can occur through (Wright, 2017).

Although we can draw many points from the academia investigated throughout this essay, we must remember that previous research that has been conducted around the discipline of family structure, its connected themes and delinquency, shows time and time again that there is great confusion in the findings of research pieces due to improper variables and a lack of adequate questioning from the research produced (Nystul, 1976). Therefore, from a criminological outlook as criminologists, family structure and delinquency should be a contemporary researching area as cotemporary criminologists look to shape research, information and findings around criminals, their causes for crimes, how they got to become criminals and more.

Therefore, as the family structure may be a possible cause for criminals to turn to crime from a psychological and sociological aspect, the discipline from a criminologist perspective should be further developed and researched as it is a contemporary discipline which looks to understand criminals. Ultimately, the fact that family structure and delinquency is a contemporary discipline, and it has not been researched as much, it should be considered a necessity to which researchers looking to understand criminals should dwell within more as family structure influences more than just the physical actions of an adult's life.

In relation to this, as mentioned previously, contemporary criminologists look to understand criminals and their lives. Often this is done by examining their behaviours whilst committing the crime before the crime occurred via their family life and also whilst on their sentence. They also examine their victims in terms of trends, reasons of choice and methods of committing those crimes in certain types of ways. However, recently, criminologists are aiming to understand criminals through their pre-adulthood stages which may hold cues to children or adolescents participating in delinquent behaviours later on in adulthood, criminologists look to find this information by researching individuals from pre-walking stages to young adulthood stages as this aspect of an individual's life can hold key informative causes to an individual dwelling within the criminal realm (Boudon, 2003). With regards to this, although there has been a growth in interest for examining the lives of children within their family structures in relation to delinquent behaviours, there is little research that explores the different types of children within the different types of family structures and the different types of family structures that exist, research pieces also lack the ability to provide a definition or detailed description of what an ideal family structure would look like, their social normative and purposes, their mental strengths and weakness, and there is also a lack of information on what a generic family structure can offer to an individual's life, in terms of social, mental and psychological wellness and positivity (Boudon, 2003).

To conclude, the inheritable criminal gene suggests that individuals are born criminal, although this may be depicted as the truth if an individual is taught from a young age about how to act within sociological and psychological mannerisms; however, this ideologue can be debated through the theory of rational choice (Wilson, 2002). Which implies that although one can be taught something, even from a young age, it is still their own choice to become criminalised (Wilson, 2002). The rational choice theory is also the dominant theory of the criminological world that suggests how individuals may become criminalised, which is via their own choice.

Birth order represents each child of the household with how each one may be affected by their parents' acknowledgements. The oldest is said to be less stressed and be less depressed due to being favoured the most within the household as they are firstborn; the second child is depicted as the troubled child and it is suggested that they are the most likely sibling to become criminalised; the youngest sibling is said to be not as depressed and stressed as the middle child, but may show some criminal qualities which, due to being the youngest and having more attention and care from the parents, can correct itself (Roche and Begue, 2005). Birth order suggests that a family unit is essential in one's life and a lack of it or feeling like you do not belong in your family unit, can cause distress and yearn individuals towards societies that connect with each other due to being outcasts, which in essence as being seen as inferior individuals leads one towards criminal pathways due to lack of an identity and a connection to a negative one (Roche and Begue, 2005). Birth order theories fail to recognise the importance and purpose that external relations outside the family environment may play within an individual's life (Roche and Begue, 2005). Friendships, love, work and social relations are seen as second relationships and thus ignored. Which in essence balances the scales towards birth order and magnifies the belief that middle children will be delinquent.

The abusive family suggests that if individuals encounter or witness abuse from a young age, whether that be sexual, physical or mental, a child may later copycat that behaviour as a way of grieving, but also believe that is the correct way of life (Morris, et al, 2011). They may also copy that behaviour in their adult life as a way of responding to the treatments that they were given (Morris, et al, 2011). Abusive families and the connections it may hold to criminalisation is most prominent in cases where there is an element of physical touch, sexual assault or power (Morris, et al, 2011). Like birth order, the abusive family fails to show the importance of external relations; as well as this, the abusive family academia does not acknowledge that although some may turn to criminalisation, there is also the opposite where some may become further victimised and become depressed and stressed as opposed to angry and criminal (Morris, et al, 2011).

Academia surrounding the themes has shown time and time again that there are many unanswered, unexplored and confusing conclusions throughout. This is mainly due to the questions not being asked or controlled factors being changed and thus changing the outcome of the results, thus confusing results to the same question. As well as this, academia surrounding the themes fails to acknowledge the reliability and stance of the rational choice model (Nystul, 1976).

Finally, although many aspects of family structure have been explored, the lack of exploration on the different genders, different types of family structures, the importance of external relations and the suggestion of the importance of rational choice is minimised, and thus creates minimalist arguments, thus leaving the rational choice model the dominant theory (Boudon, 2003). In light of this, we can still see that family structure has some relation to criminality; although the description and importance of the relations are unknown there is still one. In regards to the themes, they are inclined to rule under the family structure discipline and as a result of that do not subside to their own disciples; rather, they act collectively within the realm of family structures. The themes would not be able to work alone as they overlap in many agendas such as manifestos, probable causes to criminalisation and the effect of the nature vs nurture debate. Therefore, they predominantly fall under the guard of family structure, they just bring to light different aspects of how family structure can affect individuals on a normative agenda as well as suggestive agendas such as criminality.

Reference List

- Bernburg, J., Krohn, M. and Rivera, C. (2006). Official Labelling, Criminal Embeddedness, and Subsequent Delinquency. Journal of Research in Crime and Delinquency, [online] 43(1), pp.67-88. Available at: *https://journals-sagepub-com.ezproxy.bcu.ac.uk/doi/abs/10.1177/0022427805280068* [Accessed 10 Sep. 2019].

- Birmingham City University (2006). Guidelines and Procedures for Good Research Practice. [PDF] Birmingham: Birmingham City University, pp.1-17. Available at: *https://bcuassets.blob.core.windows.net/docs/bcu_guidelinesandprocedures-good-research-130403839823298271.pdf* [Accessed 8 Sep. 2019].

- Braun, V. & Clarke, V. (2006). Using Thematic Analysis in Psychology. Qualitative research in Psychology. 3 (2), 77-101.

- Bryman, A (2016). Social Research Methods. 5th ed. Oxford: Oxford University Press. 97-129.

- Boccio, C. and Beaver, K. (2017). The Influence of Family Structure on Delinquent Behaviour. Youth Violence and Juvenile Justice, [online] 17(1), pp.88-106. Available at: *https://journals.sagepub.com/doi/full/10.1177/1541204017727836#abstract* [Accessed 6 Sep. 2019].

- Boudon, R. (2003). Beyond Rational Choice Theory. Annual Review of Sociology, [online] 29(1), pp.1-21. Available at: _https:// go-gale-com.ezproxy.bcu.ac.uk/ps/i.do?p=AONE&u=uce&id=- GALE|A108278706&v=2.1&it=r&sid=summon_ [Accessed 8 Sep. 2019].

- Caulfield, L & Hill, J. (2014). Criminology research for beginner's: a student's guide. London: Routledge.

- Cuadra, L., Jaffe, A., Thomas, R. and DiLillo, D. (2014). Child maltreatment and adult criminal behaviour: Does criminal thinking explain the association? Child Abuse & Neglect, [online] 38(8), pp.1399-1408. Available at: _https://be6rg4tf5u. search.serialssolutions.com/?ctx_ver=Z39.88-2004&ctx_en- c=info%3Aofi%2Fenc%3AUTF-8&rfr_id=info%3Asid%2F- summon.serialssolutions.com&rft_val_fmt=info%3Aofi%2Ff- mt%3Akev%3Amtx%3Ajournal&rft.genre=article&rft. atitle=Child+maltreatment+and+adult+criminal+be- havior%3A+Does+criminal+thinking+explain+the+as- sociation%3F&rft.jtitle=Child+Abuse+%26+Neglect&rft. au=Cuadra%2C+Lorraine+E.%7CJaffe%2C+Anna+E.%7CTho- mas%2C+Renu%7CDiLillo%2C+David&rft.date=2014&rft. issn=0145-2134&rft.eissn=1873-7757&rft.volume=38&rft. issue=8&rft.spage=1399&rft.epage=1408&rft_id=info:- doi/10.1016%2Fj.chiabu.2014.02.005&rft.externalDocID=1_ s2_0_S0145213414000441&paramdict=en-UK_ [Accessed 6 Sep. 2019].

- Clarke, R. and Felson, M. (2017). Routine activity and rational choice. 1st ed. London: Routledge.

- COLVIN, M., CULLEN, F. and VEN, T. (2002). CO-ERCION, SOCIAL SUPPORT, AND CRIME: AN EMERGING THEORETICAL CONSENSUS*. Criminology, [online] 40(1), pp.19-42. Available at: *https:// be6rg4tf5u.search.serialssolutions.com/?ctx_ver=Z39.88- 2004&ctx_enc=info%3Aofi%2Fenc%3AUTF-8&rfr_id=in- fo%3Asid%2Fsummon.serialssolutions.com&rft_val_ fmt=info%3Aofi%2Ffmt%3Akev%3Amtx%3Ajournal&rft. genre=article&rft.atitle=COERCION%2C+SOCIAL+SUP- PORT%2C+AND+CRIME%3A+AN+EMERGING+THE- ORETICAL+CONSENSUS&rft.jtitle=Criminology&rft. au=COLVIN%2C+MARK&rft.au=CULLEN%2C+FRAN- CIS+T&rft.au=VEN%2C+THOMAS+VANDER&rft. date=2002-02-01&rft.pub=Blackwell+Publishing+Ltd&rft. issn=0011-1384&rft.eissn=1745-9125&rft.volume=40&rft. issue=1&rft.spage=19&rft.epage=42&rft_id=info:- doi/10.1111%2Fj.1745-9125.2002.tb00948.x&rft.externalDo- cID=CRIM19&paramdict=en-UK* [Accessed 10 Sep. 2019].

- Cullen, F. and Wilcox, P. (2010). Encyclopaedia of criminological theory. Thousand Oaks, Calif.: SAGE Publications.

- Davidson, T. (2016). The Gale Encyclopaedia of Children's Health: Infancy Through Adolescence, 3rd Edition. 3rd ed. [eBook] Cengage Learning: Gale, p. Available at: *http:// be6rg4tf5u.search.serialssolutions.com/?ctx_ver=Z39.88-*

2004&ctx_enc=info%3Aofi%2Fenc%3AUTF-8&rfr_id=in-fo%3Asid%2Fsummon.serialssolutions.com&rft_val_fmt=info%3Aofi%2Ffmt%3Akev%3Amtx%3Abook&rft.genre=bookitem&rft.title=The+Gale+Encyclope-dia+of+Children%27s+Health+%3A+Infancy+through+Ad-olescence%3A+A-C&rft.au=Davidson%2C+Tish&rft.atitle=Birth+Order&rft.date=2016-01-01&rft.isb-n=9781410332752&rft.spage=357&rft.epage=359&rft.exter-nalDocID=CX3630900112&paramdict=en-UK [Accessed 6 Sep. 2019].

- Eriksson, K., Hjalmarsson, R., Lindquist, M. and Sand-berg, A. (2015). The importance of family background and neighbourhood effects as determinants of crime. Jour-nal of Population Economics, [online] 29(1), pp.219-262. Available at: *https://search-proquest-com.ezproxy.bcu.ac.uk/docview/1726747935?pq-origsite=summon* [Accessed 8 Sep. 2019].

- Ferguson, C., Olson, C., Kutner, L. and Warner, D. (2010). Violent Video Games, Catharsis Seeking, Bullying, and De-linquency. Crime & Delinquency, 60(5), pp.764-784.

- Gates, L. Lineberger, R. M. Crockett, J. & Hubbard, J. (1988). Birth order and its relationship to depression, anxiety and self-concept test scores in children. The Journal of Genetic Psychology. 149 (1), 29-34.

- Graves, L.J. (2013). Biological Determinism. Available: *https://go-gale-com.ezproxy.bcu.ac.uk/ps/i.do?p=GVRL&u=uce&id=-GALE%7CCX4190600071&v=2.1&it=r&sid=summon#*. Last accessed 6th Sept 2019.

- Gustafson, C. (2010). The Effects of Birth Order on Personality. [PDF] Alfred: Alfred Adler Graduate School, pp.1-43. Available at: *https://alfredadler.edu/sites/default/files/Gustafson%20MP%202010.pdf* [Accessed 10 Sep. 2019].

- JOHNSON, R. (1986). FAMILY STRUCTURE AND DELINQUENCY: GENERAL PATTERNS AND GENDER DIFFERENCES. Criminology, [online] 24(1), pp.65-84. Available at: *http://be6rg4tf5u.search.serialssolutions.com/?ctx_ver=Z39.88-2004&ctx_enc=info%3Aofi%2Fenc%3AUTF-8&rfr_id=info%3Asid%2Fsummon.serialssolutions.com&rft_val_fmt=info%3Aofi%2Ffmt%3Akev%3Amtx%3Ajournal&rft.genre=article&rft.atitle=Family+Structure+and+Delinquency%3A+General+Patterns+and+Gender+Differences&rft.jtitle=Criminology&rft.au=JOHNSON%2C+RICHARD+E&rft.date=1986-02-01&rft.pub=Sage+Publications&rft.issn=0011-1384&rft.eissn=1745-9125&rft.volume=24&rft.issue=1&rft.spage=65&paramdict=en-UK* [Accessed 6 Sep. 2019].

- Jones, D. (2007). Psychosocial approaches to criminality. Cullompton: Willan Publishing.

- Kotin, J (1995). Getting started: An introduction to Dynamic Psychotherapy. Lanham, Maryland: A Jason Aronson Book. p83.

- LOUGHRAN, T., PATERNOSTER, R., CHALFIN, A. and WILSON, T. (2016). CAN RATIONAL CHOICE BE CON-SIDERED A GENERAL THEORY OF CRIME? EVIDENCE FROM INDIVIDUAL-LEVEL PANEL DATA. Criminology, [online] 54(1), pp.86-112. Available at: *https://be6rg4tf5u.search. serialssolutions.com/?ctx_ver=Z39.88-2004&ctx_enc=in- fo%3Aofi%2Fenc%3AUTF-8&rfr_id=info%3Asid%2Fsummon. serialssolutions.com&rft_val_fmt=info%3Aofi%2Ffmt%3Akev- %3Amtx%3Ajournal&rft.genre=article&rft.atitle=CAN+RA- TIONAL+CHOICE+BE+CONSIDERED+A+GENERAL+- THEORY+OF+CRIME%3F+EVIDENCE+FROM+IN- DIVIDUAL%E2%80%90LEVEL+PANEL+DATA&rft. jtitle=Criminology&rft.au=LOUGHRAN%2C+THOM- AS+A&rft.au=PATERNOSTER%2C+RAY&rft.au=CHAL- FIN%2C+AARON&rft.au=WILSON%2C+THEODORE&rft. date=2016-02-01&rft.issn=0011-1384&rft.eissn=1745-9125&rft. volume=54&rft.issue=1&rft.spage=86&rft.epage=112&rft_ id=info:doi/10.1111%2F1745-9125.12097&rft.externalDo- cID=CRIM12097&paramdict=en-UK* [Accessed 8 Sep. 2019].

- Merryweather, C. (2017). 15 Serial Killers Who Had the Childhood from Hell. [online] TheTalko. Available at: *https:// www.thetalko.com/15-serial-killers-who-had-the-childhood- from-hell/* [Accessed 7 Sep. 2019].

- McGrath, S., Nilsen, A. and Kerley, K. (2011). Sexual victimization in childhood and the propensity for juvenile delinquency and adult criminal behaviour: A systematic review. Aggression and Violent Behaviour, 16(6), pp.485-492.

- Morris, R., Gerber, J. and Menard, S. (2011). Social Bonds, Self-Control, and Adult Criminality. Criminal Justice and Behaviour, [online] 38(6), pp.584-599. Available at: *https://be6rg4tf5u.search.serialssolutions.com/?ctx_ver=Z39.88-2004&ctx_enc=info%3Aofi%2Fenc%3AUTF-8&r-fr_id=info%3Asid%2Fsummon.serialssolutions.com&rft_val_fmt=info%3Aofi%2Ffmt%3Akev%3Amtx%3A-journal&rft.genre=article&rft.atitle=Social+bonds%2C+-self-control%2C+and+adult+criminality%3A+a+nation-ally+representative+assessment+of+Hirschi%27s+Re-vised+Self-Control+Theory&rft.jtitle=Criminal+Justice+and+Behavior&rft.au=Mor-ris%2C+Robert+G&rft.au=Gerber%2C+Jurg&rft.au=Menard%2C+Scott&rft.date=2011-06-01&rft.pub=Sage+Publications%2C+Inc&rft.issn=0093-8548&rft.eissn=1552-3594&rft.volume=38&rft.issue=6&rft.spage=584&rft.externalDBID=BSHEE&rft.externalDo-cID=A260745282&paramdict=en-UK* [Accessed 11 Sep. 2019].

- Nystul, S. M. (1976). The effects of Birth order and Family size on self-concept. Australian Psychologist. 11 (2), 197-201.

- Parks, A. (2013). The effects of family structure on juvenile delinquency. [eBook] Tennessee: Electronic Thesis and Dissertation, pp.1-43. Available at: *https://dc.etsu.edu/cgi/view-content.cgi?article=3380&context=etd* [Accessed 6 Sep. 2019].

- Perren, S. and Hornung, R. (2005). Bullying and Delinquency in Adolescence: Victims' and Perpetrators' Family and Peer Relations. Swiss Journal of Psychology, 64(1), pp.51-64.

- Raine, A. (2008). O crime biológico: implicações para a socie-dade e para o sistema de justiça criminal. Revista de Psiqui-atria do Rio Grande do Sul, [online] 30(1), pp.5-8. Available at: *http://www.scielo.br/scielo.php?pid=S0101-81082008000100 003&script=sci_arttext&tlng=e*n [Accessed 7 Sep. 2019].

- Raine, A. (2013). The anatomy of violence. New York: Pan-theon Books.

- Roche, S & Begue, L. (2005). Birth order and youth delinquent behaviour testing the differential parental control hypothesis in a French Representative example. Psychology, Crime and Law. 1 (1), 73-85.

- Snyder, S. and Merritt, D. (2014). Do childhood experiences of neglect affect delinquency among child welfare involved youth? Children and Youth Services Review, 46, pp.64-71.

- TheBritishPsychologicalSociety (2018). Nottingham 2018 The British Psychological Society's Annual Conference. [eBook] Nottingham: The British Psychological Society, pp.1-159. Available at: *https://www.bps.org.uk/sites/bps.org.uk/files/*

Events%20-%20Files/AC2018%20Book%20of%20Abstracts.pdf
[Accessed 7 Sep. 2019].

- UKEssays (2018). The Family Structure and Delinquency Sociology Essay. [online]. Available from: *https://www.ukessays.com/essays/sociology/the-family-structure-and-delinquency-sociology-essay.php?vref=1* [Accessed 6 September 2019].

- Williams, K., Papadopoulou, V. and Booth, N. (2012). Prisoners' childhood and family backgrounds. [PDF] London: Ministry of Justice, pp.1-38. Available at: https://assets.publishing.service.gov.uk/government/uploads/system/uploads/attachment_data/file/278837/prisoners-childhood-family-backgrounds.pdf [Accessed 7 Sep. 2019].

- Wilson, J (2002). "Criminal Genes". Popular Mechanics. Gale Academic OneFile, *https://link.gale.com/apps/doc/A93347581/AONE?u=uce&sid=AONE&xid=804ebff2*. [Accessed 6 Sept 2019]

- Wright, K. (2017). Family Life and Delinquency and Crime. [eBook] New York: U.S. Department of Justice, pp.1-61. Available at: *https://www.ncjrs.gov/pdffiles1/Digitization/140517NCJRS.pdf* [Accessed 6 Sep. 2019].

www.ingramcontent.com/pod-product-compliance
Lightning Source LLC
Chambersburg PA
CBHW030852270326
41928CB00008B/1344